The Place of
the Sciences of Man
in the System of Sciences

The Place of
the Sciences of Man
in the System of Sciences

Jean Piaget

HARPER TORCHBOOKS
Harper & Row, Publishers
New York, Evanston, San Francisco, London

This essay was originally published as the Introduction to *Main Trends of Research in the Social and Human Sciences*, Part 1, Mouton/UNESCO, 1970. It has been slightly revised to conform to American usage and is here reprinted by arrangement with UNESCO.

THE PLACE OF THE SCIENCES OF MAN IN THE SYSTEM OF THE
SCIENCES

First HARPER TORCHBOOK edition published 1974.

LIBRARY OF CONGRESS CATALOG CARD NUMBER: 73–22612

STANDARD BOOK NUMBER: 06–131832–9

Designed by Ann Scrimgeour

Contents

This essay deals with the epistemological characteristics of the sciences of man in terms of their objectivity, of the means of observing or experimenting in them, and of the relationships they establish between theory and experience. We shall examine their links with the natural sciences, with the philosophies, and with the principal current ideological and cultural trends. But in the very first place it behooves us to explain exactly what we understand by the "sciences of man" and therefore to begin with an attempted classification.

I
The Classification of
Social Disciplines and "Human Sciences"

The distribution of disciplines among university faculties varies greatly from one country to another and cannot be used as a basis for classification. We shall confine ourselves here to pointing out that no distinction can be drawn between the disciplines frequently referred to as the "social sciences" and those known as the "human sciences," since social phenomena clearly depend upon all human characteristics, including psychophysiological processes, while reciprocally the human sciences are all social, viewed from one angle or another. Such a distinction could only make sense (and that is the assumption on which it was based) if it were possible to dissociate in man what pertains to the particular society in which he lives from what is common to the whole of humanity. Many thinkers, of course, remain favorable to such a distinction, tending to oppose inborn traits to those acquired in a given physical or social environment, so that "human nature" is seen to rest upon the sum of hereditary characteristics. But the idea is fast gaining ground that the innate consists mainly in abilities to function, irrespective of inherited, ready-prepared structures[1] (unlike the instincts, most of which are hereditarily "programmed"): speech, for instance, is acquired socially but is related to a brain center (Broca's convolution); if this center is damaged before the faculty of speech has been acquired, other cortical areas not intended for that use will take over

[1] The return to the hypothesis of the innate by the linguist Chomsky should, however, be noted, although his theories would remain just as valid if this "innate fixed nucleus" were replaced by a self-regulating mechanism resulting from sensorimotor development at the stage of incipient self-expression.

its functions. Nothing therefore prevents us from concluding that, contrary to the ideas prevailing in Rousseau's day, the need to belong to a particular society is one of the essential parts of "human nature," with the result that there is a growing trend toward doing away with any distinction between the sciences known as "social" and those known as "human."

On the other hand, other subdivisions must necessarily be made in the wide range of disciplines that relate to man's multitudinous activities; for the present essay will deal only with a limited number of them, and only with those that can be called "nomothetic," or "law-seeking." But not every study bearing upon man or society sets itself such a task. We shall therefore attempt to reduce these disciplines to four main groups, it being understood from the outset that this classification, as is usual, includes some typical examples but also a somewhat smaller number of borderline cases that constitute bridges between the clear-cut categories.

I.

We shall name *nomothetic sciences* those disciplines that are concerned with identifying "laws," sometimes in the sense of quantitative relations that are comparatively constant and can be expressed in the form of mathematical functions, but also in the sense of plain factual information or ordinal relations, structural analyses, and so on, which can be described in everyday language or in more or less formalized language (logic, etc.).

Scientific psychology, sociology, ethnology, linguistics, economics, and demography clearly fall into the category of "law-seeking" disciplines in the wide sense described above. A psychologist may, of course, study individual cases and work on differential psychology, the linguist may study a particular language or launch into typology, and so forth. But, however narrowly confined the field of research may be, the work itself is still concerned with comparison and classification aiming at generalization and at the identification of laws, even if the laws in question are only related to questions of frequency, distribution, or range of variations (and even if, for reasons of prudence, the use of the term "laws" is avoided).

In addition, it goes without saying that under each of these disciplines, research bears in part on phenomena disposed in a diachronic order, that is to say, having a "history." Thus in linguistics, a study among others may be undertaken on the history of languages, or in so-called "genetic" psychology the development of behavior may be investigated, and so on. It is on this historical plane, which is of fundamental importance in many cases, that some sectors of the nomothetic sciences meet some of those we shall below call the historical sciences. Some differences are nevertheless to be found between these diachronic researches, proper to the nomothetic disciplines, and similar research in historical disciplines, although naturally intermediate positions can always be found. In the case of individual development (language, intelligence, and so on) historical changes are repeated in each generation and can therefore involve experimental controls and even a variation of factors, in such a way that the main objective remains the seeking of laws, in this case the "laws of development." In research on collective historical changes, such as the development of languages, economic structures, and so on, law-seeking is still to be found, whether the purpose is to explain a given general structure by reference to its past (which brings us back to the laws of development) or, on the contrary, to explain previous historical facts (such as interest rates on an ancient market) by means of synchronistic laws currently verifiable.

A second basic characteristic, as important as the identification or discovery of laws that is proper to the nomothetic sciences, distinguishes these from the three categories II, III, and IV, that we shall examine later: it is the use of experimental research methods— whether of a rigorous nature such as those used, for instance, in biology (and which are found to be essential today in most areas of scientific psychological research), or of a broader nature as in systematic observation supported by statistical verification, the analysis of "variances," the control of implicit relations (analysis of counterexamples), and so forth. We shall discuss the methodological problems of the nomothetic sciences of man later (in Chapters 3 and 4); but the methods of verification, whether simple or complex, whereby schematic theories are controlled by factual experience, constitute the most general distinctive characteristic of these disciplines as compared with those described below.

A third basic characteristic must be added to the two preceding ones, namely, the tendency to focus research on a limited number of variables at a time. Naturally it is not always possible to isolate factors, as in physics (and this comment holds good from biology onward), although some statistical processes (analysis of variances) may in some cases allow for the respective influences of several variables to be judged. But between the natural sciences, whose experimental methods allow for a clear separation of variables, and the historical sciences, in which the variables are sometimes inextricably entangled, the nomothetic sciences of man have at their disposal intermediary strategies with aims closer to those of the first group.

II.

We shall call *historical sciences* those disciplines the purpose of which is to reconstitute and interpret the unfolding of all manifestations of social life across time. Whether concerned with the life of individuals whose actions have left a mark on the society they lived in, of their works, of ideas that may have exerted a lasting influence, of techniques and sciences, of literature and the arts, of philosophy and religions, of institutions, of economic and other exchanges, and of civilization in general, history deals with everything that affects collective life, whether it can be examined singly or as part of a complex.

The question that arises immediately is that of determining whether or not the historical sciences form a separate unit with its own clear and distinct characteristics, or whether they simply represent the diachronic side of each of the nomothetic, legal, or philosophical disciplines. This essay is not concerned with trends but with the current status of the questions dealt with. We therefore do not need to consider whether the historical sciences are only of ephemeral value, ultimately to be absorbed into the other categories, but simply to explain why this paper, while constantly stressing the importance of the diachronic dimension of phenomena, will nevertheless draw a distinction between the historical and the nomothetic sciences and finally deal only with the latter, since history itself appears today to show certain specific and comparatively stable characteristics.

Even though every kind of link is to be found between the nomothetic and the historical analysis of unfolding phenomena or events in time, there does seem to be a fairly marked difference between them due to a complementary relationship in their approach to the temporal sequence of events. Four main factors may be observed in this connection: (a) determinations due to developments (development consisting of a regular or even sequential series of qualitative transformations resulting in a progressive structuring); (b) determinations arising from synchronic self-balancing due to built-in dynamics; (c) interference or haphazard events; and (d) individual or collective "decisions." Now when the nomothetic disciplines examine a temporal series of events, whether styled "historical" or not, their efforts are constantly directed toward the identification of laws and consequently toward the necessary elimination of variables to achieve that result. They will thus endeavor to find sequential laws (a), or laws of equilibrium (b); in the case of haphazard phenomena (c), they will not deal with isolated cases that defy classification but examine mass effects with a view to arriving at conjectural laws; in the case of decisions (d), they will deal less with their content than with their processing so far as it can be analyzed on a probabilist basis (theory of games or decision). The historian's purpose, on the contrary, although complementary (even if, as today, he uses all the nomothetic data) is not that of abstracting variables with a view to the identification of laws, but to grasp each historical process in its complexity and consequently in its original and irreducible meaning. When a given development (a) or self-balancing of events (b) occurs, the historian, even if interested in the underlying laws insofar as they help him to understand the meaning of the event, is seeking the particular characteristics involved, precisely because they, rather than the law, are particular to the event. As far as haphazard events (c) are concerned, it goes without saying that the historian deals with their individual content that, although impossible to calculate, can be reconstituted, such reconstitution being in fact one of the historian's tasks. In the same way, it is the content of decisions (d) that are of principal interest to historians, representing as they do the continuing renewal of the history of humanity in the form of response to specific situations (an inextricable mixture of determination and chance (a) and (c)).

In short, however close the link between the nomothetic and the historical sciences may be, and however dependent one may be on the other, their aims are complementary and therefore separate even when they are dealing with the same subject: the need to *abstract* in the first corresponds to the need to *reconstitute* reality in the second, the latter being quite as primordial a function in the understanding of mankind but distinct from that of identifying laws.

It is true that the term "the laws of history" is often used; but when it is not invoked as a metaphor to further political ends, it is used with reference to standard cycles, as in sociology (the phases of revolutions, for example), economics, and so on. In the latter cases, the cycles observed enter ipso facto into the field of particular nomothetic sciences, the methods of which can naturally be applied by the historian himself, acting as a sociologist or economist, etc., these methods being quite different from those of mere observation or reconstitution already referred to and providing the only means of carrying out the necessary verifications. In this connection, we should draw attention to a broad contemporary trend to consider history as a science based on quantification and structures (F. Braudel, J. Kruithof, J. Craebeckx, O. Lebran, and so on),[2] an idea that opens up many interesting possibilities, but that would today turn history into the diachronic side of sociology and economics, although it might in the future transform the historical disciplines in such a way as to make their main purpose that of working out a synthesis of the diachronic dimensions of all the human sciences.

In addition, many branches of history are of course closely concerned with the study of more or less autonomous developments in the sense defined above. The history of the sciences provides one example, and the history of mathematics holds an exceptional place within that framework by virtue of its inherent characteristics of progressive structuring. It thus meets on a common ground the central problems of the psychology of intelligence, of the sociogenesis of the acquisition of knowledge, and of scientific epistemology.

---

[2] We should also mention G. Beaujouan's study "Le temps historique" in *L'histoire et ses méthodes* (Paris, Gallimard, Encyclopédie de la Pléiade), which studies historical rhythms and cycles.

III.

The *legal sciences* are set apart by the fact that the norms that, grouped together, form the laws they are concerned with differ fundamentally from the more or less general relationships forming the "laws" dealt with by the nomothetic sciences. A norm is not set by the identification of existing relationships. It belongs to a quite separate category of what might be described as "duties" (*sollen*). It thus lays down obligations and attributions that remain valid even if violated or not observed, whereas a natural law is based on causal determinism or conjectural reasoning and its validity depends exclusively on its agreement with facts.

Although this is a very clear-cut distinction, a borderline area exists in which the legal sciences as such and the other sciences meet. The history of law, insofar as it deals with the history of legal institutions (not to mention the history of theories), can no longer, of course, be considered as a normative discipline, but rather as an analysis of realities that were—and sometimes still are—recognized as norms by the societies involved, while at the same time constituting historical facts, for the legal historian among others. This dual point of view, in which the central fact, whether past or present, is considered as a norm by the subject and an event by the observer, is even more clearly seen in one of the truly nomothetic disciplines, legal sociology, in which legal behavior is studied from the point of view of social phenomena. The purpose of legal sociology, unlike legal science, is not to study normative values but, and this is quite different, to analyze the social phenomena involved in the establishment and the working of such norms. The term "normative facts" has been happily introduced into the general vocabulary of this discipline by its specialists to describe that which constitutes a norm for the subject and, at the same time, an object of analysis for the observer engaged in studying both the behavior of the subject and the norms he recognizes as objective facts. This concept has general application, as in the study of ethics, where the sociologist is not concerned with the validity of the norms accepted by the subjects but seeks to discover the process that has led them to consider themselves bound to observe those norms. In the same way, "normative facts" are studied in genetic psychology when the question is to discover how subjects who were originally insensitive to certain logical norms come to regard them as essentials through a process depending partly on their life in the community and partly on the internal structuration of the action envisaged. In short, although the legal field may generally be considered as normative, it is found to give rise, as in the other nomothetic fields, to factual studies and causal analyses of individual or collective behavior related to the given norms, and such studies are then necessarily of a nomothetic nature.

In particular, when a legal school considers that the *sollen* of a norm of law does no more than express the will of the state and through it that of the social forces or classes governing the society, the law cannot be included in the category of *must be,* but belongs to the field of purely material relations that can be studied objectively. For those concerned with norms, however, this would belong to legal sociology.[3]

IV.

Finally we come to the group of *philosophical disciplines,* which are particularly difficult to classify, if only because of the lack of agreement among its proponents as to the scope and extent, and even the unity, of the various branches usually included under this heading.

The only statement that cannot be challenged, since it appears to be common to all schools of thought, is that the purpose of philosophy is to attain a general coordination of human values, that is to say, a concept of the world that takes into account not only acquired knowledge and a critical evaluation of such knowledge, but also the sum of man's multitudinous convictions and values in every context. Philosophy therefore goes further than the objective sciences and places them in relation to a group of evaluations and meanings ranging from customs to metaphysics in the strict sense.

The divergences of opinion start from the point at which the nature of this postulate is studied in relation to the totality of reality.

[3] Other examples of relations between the legal sciences and research on various other categories, in particular, logic, are provided in my *Main Trends in Interdisciplinary Research* (New York: Harper & Row, Publishers, Harper Torchbooks, 1973).

For certain thinkers, philosophy is essentially a form of wisdom, a "setting into motion," as Jaspers says, whereas all clearly established knowledge obviously falls into the field of specialized learning in the strictest sense of science. For others, including several dialecticians, the study of philosophy calls above all for awareness of dialectical processes arising from "science on the march" and from a commitment to take options. For others, finally, like Husserl, philosophy attains real wisdom, higher than scientific knowledge—although positivism and several nonpositivist writers contest that possibility from an epistemological point of view.

We need not enter into the debate at this point (it will in any case be referred to in Chapter 5 in connection with the relationship between the nomothetic sciences and philosophical trends), but shall confine ourselves to determining which disciplines may be classified as philosophical as opposed to nomothetic among the sciences of man. This division of disciplines, however, is precisely the problem we face, for the reasons already given and mainly because of a historical process, initiated in the nineteenth century and gaining more and more ground today: the splitting off of a number of branches, originally philosophical, into autonomous and specialized disciplines. This was the case of sociology and particularly of psychology, as we shall see shortly in connection with the history of the nomothetic sciences. But it was also the case for logic; and today it largely holds good for scientific epistemology. For on the one hand, modern logic has turned into a quasi-mathematical discipline, with its own methods and a field of research independent of any metaphysical considerations; and on the other hand, each of the natural and human sciences tends to work out its own epistemology, which is more closely linked with that of the other disciplines than it is concerned with metaphysical speculation.

But the most difficult problem raised in connection with these two branches of learning is that of determining their position in relation to the scientific disciplines in general and to the nomothetic sciences of man in particular. On the one hand, scientific learning is undoubtedly a human activity, and although logic and scientific epistemology contribute essential and verifiable information without necessarily involving philosophy in its traditional, academic sense, it goes without saying that the nomothetic sciences of man are also closely concerned with those two disciplines. In particular, a close relationship is to be found between research on the psychogenesis of intelligence and what has been called genetic epistemology, that is, the study of the process of learning as it develops. But on the other hand, logic, whose processes are essentially self-evident, is closer to mathematics than to any other discipline, and scientific epistemology has so far won its laurels only in the fields of mathematics and physics. These new disciplines should therefore be seen as one link among many others between the sciences of man and the natural sciences or deductive disciplines, and this together with other factors clearly shows how complex is the relationship between the nomothetic sciences of man and the overall system of sciences.

Nevertheless and despite the many intermediate stages we have noted by way of example, the division of the various sciences and disciplines into the four categories mentioned above seems to correspond to the present state of knowledge and gives the nomothetic sciences of man a natural and relatively independent status.

2

Major Trends in the
History of the Nomothetic Sciences

The purpose of this study is not to provide a historical background for the nomothetic sciences of man, which can be found in many other works. However, in order to bring out the main present trends in these sciences, some basic facts are needed, and it may prove useful to recall their historical antecedents, in other words, the past trends from which the present movements are descended, either directly or by way of reaction.

The problem can be stated in the following terms: Ever since the first thinkers and teaching systems, there have always been discussions on psychology, linguistics, sociology, and economics. The *Germania* of Tacitus, for instance, touches on cultural anthropology, while geographers in every age have had to consider demographic problems. In general there has always been speculation and commentary on the activities of man, and every philosophical system has in some respect outlined or adumbrated the specialized disciplines with which we are here concerned. But systematic or episodic speculation is one thing, while the formation of a science as such, with a list of specifically defined problems and its own sophisticated methods, is another. To put it more precisely, there is all the difference between a dissertation and a process of observation and—more important—of verification. The problem is then to analyze the factors that have brought the present disciplines from the prescientific stage to the state, or at least the ideal, of the nomothetic sciences. Five such factors can be distinguished:

I.

The first is the tendency toward comparison, which is far from being as generalized and natural as might be supposed. The two most ready tendencies of spontaneous thought, and even of speculation at its initial stages, are to assume that one stands at the center of the world, both spiritual and material, and to elevate one's own rules or even habits into universal standards. The construction of a science can in no way be founded upon such an initial centering with further knowledge simply piled on by addition; the additive process must also be systematic, and the prerequisite for objective systematization is decentering away from the personal point of view that was dominant at the start. The comparative approach brings about this decentering, while at the same time broadening the law-seeking process to the point where the knowledge becomes amenable to a variety of reference systems.

This comparative approach emerges particularly clearly in the history of linguistics, which dates back two or three thousand years and which witnessed many attempts at systematization before the present age (cf., for example, the semantic efforts made in the Middle Ages). Speculation on the meaning of words begins at the teaching stage, and it is therefore legitimate to ask why the creation of scientific linguistics has not come about faster or more purposefully. The answer is clearly that, in the early stages, speculation on words as such remained subject to two forms of subjectivism: psychological, until many other terms of comparison emerge; and legalistic, that is, leading people to believe that the science of language is no more than grammar, and that the grammar of a language is a more or less direct reflection of universal logic.

Teaching of the humanities did, of course, bring about some degree of decentering together with the notion of the historical descents of languages (cf. Chapter 1, Section 11). In addition to his *Grammaire de Port-Royal,* Lancelot also produced a work entitled *Jardin des racines grecques,* but the title alone of his joint study with Arnauld, *Grammaire générale et raisonnée,* provides sufficient proof of the law-seeking centering just referred to.[4] F. Bopp's strictly comparative approach in his *Grammaire comparée des langues indo-européennes* is the first real example of the decentering essential to a scientific approach, and we can readily understand why it came so late.

A very similar phenomenon is evident in sociology, where the first speculations on society were dominated both by an obsession with the social cell, derived from a very long tradition, and by legalistic preoccupations that failed to distinguish between sociology and politics—and this does not mean that greater objectivity in sociology cannot have political implications. The comparative and decentered approach is so difficult in this case that Rousseau, seeking examples for his speculation on the social phenomenon in primitive rather than civilized behavior (which represents a considerable advance over the ideas of his time), thought up the "noble savage"—an individual existing before society, but upon whom he conferred, without realizing it, all the characteristics of morality, rationality, and even legalistic deduction that sociology has since taught us to be the products of community life. This noble savage is the product of an imagination that is so barely decentered that it bears an astonishingly close likeness to Rousseau himself composing the *Social Contract*. The same phenomenon reappeared in the middle of the nineteenth century when one of the founders of cultural anthropology, Tylor, in order to explain the animism peculiar to "primitive" civilization, invented a "philosophical savage" who reasons about dreams, sickness, and death very much after the fashion of an Anglo-Saxon empiricist placed in the state of ignorance of a noncivilized man but speculating in the manner of Hume and his peers. Nevertheless, Tylor took a great step forward when, through his efforts to collect not just ideas but facts, he hit upon the comparative approach.

This was the direction, i.e., decentration in relation to immediate social experience, which was followed by the founders of modern sociology in the nineteenth century. There is no need for us here to

---

[4] It should be noted that N. Chomsky considers himself a descendant of the Port-Royal grammarians because (no doubt rightly) he is more inclined to see the effect of logic on language than the converse. But the very fact that he adds to the "fixed kernel" of grammar a series of transforming processes of which he has discovered the existence and laws shows what progress had been made toward decentration.

assess the success or inadequacy of their efforts, which were followed by many others. Thus the purpose of Comte's *Law of the Three States* is to detach scientific thought from the level of collective representation and to situate it in relation to other intellectual attitudes.

The Marxist system consists in a vast effort to situate ideologies in relation to social classes, Durkheim's aim is to situate our collective representations in relation to the elementary stages of sociogenesis, and so on. In each of these instances, the chief decentering action consists in ceasing to take individual thought as the source of collective reality, and in considering the individual as the product of a social process.

The decentering process that psychology had to undergo before it could become a science was of a different kind, but also led to comparative approaches. Under the influence of law-seeking tendencies, philosophical psychology was centered on the ego as the immediate expression of the soul, and the method, which seemed adequate at that stage, was that of introspection. After a long process involving systematic comparisons between the normal and the pathological, between adult and child, man and animal, and so forth, the general position that eventually came to prevail in scientific psychology was that conscience can be understood only when placed within the context of "conduct," which implies methods of observation and experiment that will be discussed later.

If we compare the many developments of macroeconomics (and of microeconomics, to which we shall revert in connection with the theory of games) in the early days of economic science with Adam Smith's *Inquiry into the Nature and Causes of the Wealth of Nations* or, in more general terms, Rousseau's *Discours sur l'origine et les fondements de l'inégalité,* we cannot help being struck by the decentration that has taken place since the time of that abstraction, *homo oeconomicus*—an image of the individual in certain restricted and very specialized social situations. Whether in the Marxist doctrine of alienation, the probabilistic and statistical analyses of Keynes, or modern econometrics, we cannot fail to notice this basic phenomenon of the comparative and centrifugal approach.

It should also be pointed out that this phenomenon, which makes for increased objectivity in sociology and economics, is often dependent on the evolution of society itself. For instance, the problem of social classes (which was noticed by Thierry, Mignet, and Guizot as early as at the beginning of the nineteenth century) only achieved its full expression in the light of the well-known economic transformations that took place later.

II.

Several of the examples just quoted show that a second trend must necessarily be added to the first: the *historical* or *genetic* tendency. One of the main differences between the prescientific stage of our disciplines and their establishment as autonomous and methodical sciences lies in the gradual discovery that directly experienced individual or social states that appear to give rise to intuitive or immediate knowledge are in fact the product of a historical process or development that has to be known before its results can be understood. This is again a form of decentration, in a sense, but in addition to providing an opportunity for comparison, it also offers a means of explanation insofar as the developments in question are related causally.

Linguistics was naturally the first of the sciences of man to benefit from this historical approach, since enough of the text of the mother languages has been preserved in written documents to make it possible to reconstruct the history of the principal modern civilized languages. The links are sufficiently obvious to have led very early, even in the absence in certain cases of proved methods, to etymological research, which seemed to be the basis of linguistic science long before de Saussure systematically distinguished between synchronic and diachronic questions.

Being based on history, sociology has likewise had access to numerous documents concerning the past of our societies and civilizations. Nevertheless, in this field where facts are relatively accessible, it is surprising to note that the problem of evolution was not grasped until a late stage, owing to the fact that all attention was initially focused on the supposedly unchanging nature of man and the standards governing social life, also regarded as an equally constant emanation of human nature. Following in the wake of certain predecessors, including perhaps Comenius[5] and Vico, Hegel was no

[5] Whose quasi-evolutionist ideas were the product of his neoplatonism, as has recently been demonstrated by workers in Prague.

doubt the first to perceive, on a still essentially conceptual rather than factual basis, the sociological dimension of history, by applying dialectics to the process of social change. It is hardly necessary to recall how Marx developed this trend, but that he did so by advancing from the concept to the facts and by generalizing the application of the historical dialectic to economic structures and to the sociological analysis of ideologies.

One of the decisive factors in the establishment of the human sciences along genetic lines was the discovery, or rediscovery, by Darwin of the evolution of organized species. For it follows logically that if man is no longer regarded as an immutable creation with an absolute beginning, all the problems connected with his activities must be reframed in completely new terms. No longer able to refer back to an initial condition including, in planned or predetermined form, all the compulsive factors that determine human nature, inquirers found themselves confronted with questions of causal explanation, which obliged them to consider through what actual factors the human species, as distinct from the animal, had come to construct languages, societies, and a mental life, to create techniques and an economic organization, in short, to father those innumerable structures of which only the existence and most obvious functions had hitherto been known. From then on the problem was to understand how they had come about. Even if the origins of this historical process are lost in the mists of human paleontology, every question of transformation, both past and present, takes on a new meaning in the evolutionary context, since it calls for an explanatory analysis. Comte's positivist doctrine, which failed to take account of the evolutionary teachings of Lamarck and was propounded before Darwin, could reduce the scientific ideal to the mere function of forecasting on the basis of laws. The problem now, in the light of evolutionary theory, is to reach a much deeper understanding of the "mode of production" of phenomena, condemned by Comte but indefatigably pursued by the nomothetic sciences of man and the natural sciences.

While Darwin's evolutionary theory undoubtedly influenced sociology, and in particular Spencer, its effect on scientific psychology was even more direct, since mental activity and behavior are more closely linked to organic states. Darwin himself is one of the founders of comparative psychology through his studies on the expression of the emotions. In human psychology, while we know very little about the intellectual and emotional functions of prehistoric man, being familiar only with his techniques, the concept of evolution gave rise to that kind of "mental embryology" that is child psychology, not forgetting its close relations with psychopathology, which is the study of the disintegrations matching the integrations that accompany development. This is the reason why, in the United States at the end of the nineteenth century, the study of the formation of mental structures in children was known as "genetic psychology."

III.

A third determining influence in the development of the sciences of man was the model offered by the natural sciences. Two different types of factors must here be distinguished. The first is the influence exerted by positivist philosophy and the various forms of metaphysical scientism current in the nineteenth century, when the climate might have seemed favorable to the general extension of the scientific spirit to all branches of knowledge. It was against this background that Taine, for instance, attempted to base literary criticism on naturalist considerations and wrote a work, *On Intelligence,* in which he sought to reduce intelligence to a "polyp tree of images." In fact, this philosophic factor has tended more toward a general attitude or motivation of belittlement than to detailed objective research. On the other hand, a second factor, more or less bound up with the first in some authors but quite distinct in others, consists in the influence of the "models" used in the natural sciences, the success of which led people to wonder whether they might not be utilized with similar good results in the sciences of man.

The early stages of experimental psychology in the field of perception provide a clear example. The physiology of the nervous system offers a variety of processes in which an external stimulant triggers off a reaction; the sequences can be analyzed both qualitatively and quantitively. In cases where the reaction is accompanied by such states of consciousness as sensations or perceptions, it was obviously necessary to attempt an objective evaluation and to determine the exact relationship between the physical stimulus and the way in which it was perceived. This led to "psychophysics," many of whose results are still valid today: a trail was blazed in the middle of the nineteenth century by such men as Weber, Fechner, Helmholtz, Hering, and many others that is still not exhausted and whose basic problem remains the coordination of physiology and psychological analysis.

In the same way, Galton's anthropometrics raised general problems of measurement involving methods of statistical analysis and correlation, and this effort can be taken as one of the starting points of the techniques of testing.

We shall pursue this matter no further at the present stage, since Chapter 6 deals with the general problem of the relationship between the sciences of man and the natural sciences. It may be noted here, however, that while the first effects of this convergence were characterized mainly by a tendency to reduce the new problems, the later stages in the historical development of this research showed, first, that the use of models taken from the natural sciences in no way precluded consideration of the specificity of higher phenomena; and second, that several of the techniques developed in the field of the sciences of man had a reverse influence on the biological and even the psychochemical disciplines. As early as the nineteenth century, Darwin's ideas on selection were partly suggested by economic and demographic concepts and not just by the artificial selection methods of stockbreeders.

IV.

The essential factor in the scientific development of subjects that, like psychology and sociology, broke away from the original common trunk of philosophy, was the tendency toward the delimitation of problems, with the methodological demands that this implies. Positivism considers—and this is its chief originality—that unchanging frontiers mark the boundaries of science, thus making it possible to distinguish by their very natures between scientific and philosophical or metaphysical problems. In fact, an examination of historical developments leads to two sets of conclusions. The first is that these frontiers are constantly shifting and that the sciences are always infinitely "open." For instance, introspection by the subject himself into his own consciousness was considered inadmissible by

Comte and classified under metaphysics (hence the absence of psychology from Comte's classification of the sciences). A little over half a century later, the Würzburg school in Germany and A. Binet in France made systematic use of induced introspection to demonstrate that thought cannot be reduced to mental images but consists in acts in the truest sense. This opened the way to a linking of intelligence and action and to a psychology of conduct that, although it assigns a limited role to introspection, does so after a long series of systematic experiments that furnish "objective" grounds for these limitations instead of purely arbitrary decisions.

The second basic conclusion is that, while frontier shifts between philosophy and the sciences do not depend on an a priori division of problems, precise reasons can be given for these progressive delimitations, along the following lines. Since philosophy attempts to encompass the whole of reality, it necessarily bears two characteristics that constitute its true originality. The first consists in not dissociating questions one from another, since its specific purpose is to aim at the whole. The second is that, in the attempt to coordinate all human activities, each philosophical position implies evaluation and commitment, which excludes the possibility of any general meeting of minds to the extent that the values involved are unshakable (for example, spirituality or materialism, and so on). It is from this point of view that the spiritualist introspection of Maine de Biran and Victor Cousin was unacceptable to Comte, who was therefore right to regard it as a metaphysical problem, since its avowed purpose was to justify concepts such as liberty, that is, beliefs on which agreement could not be, or had not been, reached. Science, on the other hand, begins as soon as a problem can be isolated in such a way as to relate its solution to investigations that are universally accessible and verifiable, dissociating them from questions of evaluation or conviction. This does not mean that these definable problems are known in advance, since only experience will show whether the attempt can succeed. However, it does imply an effort to find a demarcation that may meet with general agreement: by using introspection to determine the relations between judgment and a mental image, and by setting to one side the problems of liberty or the nature of the soul, the Würzburg school and Binet were using a clearly defined and hence scientific method. The records show that they were in agreement, which is all the more striking when one considers that at the beginning there was no contact between the German and French scholars.

In short, sciences such as psychology, sociology, and logic became detached from philosophy not because their problems were established once and for all as scientific and of no concern to philosophy, or even less with a view to gaining for themselves a sort of advance guarantee of greater accuracy, but simply because progress toward greater knowledge requires that problems should be identified and that those on which no agreement is possible at a given moment should be set aside and all attention focused on subjects in which joint investigation and verification are possible. Separation or differentiation from the initial common trunk may be achieved peacefully, as in the case of logic, which, in its own deductive and algebraic field, immediately found its own methods and autonomy—a process simplified by the fact that the uninitiated found it somewhat difficult to follow. In other cases, declarations of independence have been more explosive, for example, in psychology, in which everyone believes himself competent, with the result that specialized research work was not at first recognized as valid and authoritative. Whatever the occasion, the process is set in motion by similar principles of specialization arising from the need for agreement based on the use of common and converging methods.

V.

The fifth decisive factor in the formation of the nomothetic sciences of man therefore relates to the choice of such methods. At a later stage (Chapter 4) we shall consider their specific characteristics, but what should be emphasized now, in the context of these methods' historical origins, is their general and decisive role as instruments of verification. A science can only begin to function when there is an adequate definition of the problems circumscribing a research field in which a meeting of minds can be achieved, and we have just seen that this was how the sciences that had to break away from metaphysics came into being. But what is the nature of this meeting of minds, and by what criterion did the champions of an emergent science conclude that they had succeeded in establishing a consensus different in kind from those that unite the members of a school of philosophy or of a political or artistic group? The criterion is by no means static, since there can be much more discussion and disagreement among experimenters concerned with the same question than among the disciples of the founder of a speculative doctrine. The rallying point of the sciences with which we are concerned, during their formative period, was a common desire for verification, the accuracy of which increased in relation to the degree of mutual checks and even criticisms.

Speculation and intuition are the only methods of approach in subjects involving basic value judgments and commitments. The essence of any attempt to isolate a problem in order to detach it from subjective or emotional convictions is the search for a common ground of verification—experimental verification in the broad sense in cases of fact, or numerical and formal verification in deductive disciplines such as logic. Naturally, all the great philosophical systems, side by side with their speculative elements, abound in precise observations or factual data; more important still, the great philosophers of the past have almost all been innovators in the natural or human sciences. Nevertheless the scientific phase of research begins when, after separating what is verifiable from what is speculative or intuitive, the research worker fashions special methods, adapted to his problem and at one and the same time methods of approach and of verification.

This factor, together with its forerunners, seems to us to account for the historical developments that have marked the birth and growth of the nomothetic sciences of man.

3

Special Epistemological Features
and Foundations of the Sciences of Man

Generally speaking, the experimental sciences appeared on the scene much later than the disciplines based on deduction. The Greeks developed their own mathematics and logic, and sought to resolve astronomical problems; but even with the promising speculations of the pre-Socratic philosophers and the findings of Archimedes himself, it was not possible until modern times to build up physics in a fully experimental sense. There are at least three reasons why experimentation lagged behind deduction, and they are also of direct interest to the epistemology of the sciences of man, though their nature is even more complicated.

I.

The first reason is that the natural tendency of the mind[6] is to perceive reality intuitively and to make deductions, but not experiments; for unlike deduction, experimentation is not a free or even a direct, spontaneous product of intelligence; it calls for acceptance of external authorities requiring a much more extensive, and psychologically more exacting, process of adaptation.

---

[6] By this is meant the spontaneous propensities observed in any objective study of the growth of the mental faculties. With children (irrespective of what they may have learned at school or from adults), it has been noted that deductive processes develop long before experimental ones, and that the latter are manifestly subordinated to the higher forms of deduction. Facts of this kind, which can be fully and easily verified, show that socioeconomic factors, which generally play a significant role, cannot adequately explain why experimentation develops later than deduction.

The second reason, a logical extension of the first, is that in the field of deduction the earliest or most elementary mind processes are also the simplest: associating, dissociating, arranging asymmetrical relations in a given order, linking up symmetries, establishing analogies, and so on. The experimental field is quite different: its raw material is highly complex, and the preliminary problem is always to isolate the components from the tangled mass. In the domain of physics it took the genius of a Galileo to work out simple movements that could be expressed in equations, remembering that the fall of a leaf or the drifting of a cloud are extremely intricate in terms of measurement.

The third reason, basically even more important, is that the so-called "reading" of an experiment is never merely a reading, but implies an active dealing with reality, since it means the dissociation of elements, and thus calls for building a logical or mathematical structure. In other words, it is impossible to arrive at the experimental fact without a logico-mathematical framework. Thus it is a natural—if frequently ignored—requirement that a certain number of deductive patterns must exist before one can attempt or succeed in making experiments.

These three reasons are even more applicable to the sciences of man; indeed, they take on additional force as a result of the greater complexity of the problems involved and above all of the seemingly much more immediate nature of the insights into the subject—all of which retards the need for systematic experimentation. The result was that the tendency to deduce and to speculate outweighed for a much longer time the need to experiment, that the separation of the various factors was and remains much more difficult, and that the logico-mathematical, qualitative, and probabilist frames of reference were much less easy to construct (and are still far from adequate). If experimental physics lagged for centuries behind mathematics, practitioners of the sciences of man need not be surprised at the time taken to get them established and must regard their present situation as a very modest beginning in relation to the work that has still to be performed, and to their legitimate expectations.

In addition to the difficulties shared by all experimental disciplines, the sciences of man are faced with an epistemological situation and with methodological problems that are largely peculiar to them and that must be closely examined. The difficulty is that the human sciences, whose object is man in his countless manifestations and which are the product of man's deliberate actions, are placed in the special position of having man both as their subject and their object, which naturally poses a series of specific and difficult problems.

It should, however, be pointed out at the outset that this situation is not entirely novel and can be paralleled in the natural sciences, in which solutions have been worked out that can sometimes be of assistance. Naturally, when physics deals with things at our common level of observation, the object may be regarded as relatively independent of the subject. It is true that this object can only be known through perceptions, which have a subjective aspect, and through calculations or metrical and logico-mathematical structurations, which are also subjective activities. But a distinction must at once be drawn between the individual subject, centered on his sense organs or his own actions—and hence on the ego or egocentric subject as a source of possible deformation or illusion of a "subjective" type, in the basic meaning of the term—and the decentered subject who coordinates his actions as between them and those of others; who measures, calculates, and deduces in a way that can be generally verified; and whose epistemic activities are therefore common to all subjects, even if they are replaced by electronic or cybernetic machines with a built-in logical and mathematical capacity similar to that of the human brain. The whole history of physics is about decentration, which reduced to a *minimum* the deformations introduced by an egocentric subject and based this science to the *maximum* on the laws of an epistemic subject—which comes back to saying that objectivity became possible and that the object was made relatively independent of the subject.

However, on the larger scale, such as that adopted under the relativity theory, the observer is influenced and modified by the phenomenon he observes, with the result that what he perceives is in reality related to his particular situation, without his being aware of it until he has undergone further decentration (for instance, Newton regarded space-time measurements taken at our own scale as universal). The solution then lies in decentration at higher levels, in other words, in coordinating the covariations inherent in the data produced by different hypothetical observers. On the microphysics scale, it is in fact well known that the intervention of the experimenter modifies the observed phenomenon (a situation reciprocal to the previous one), with the result that the "observable" is a combination including the modification introduced by the experimental activity. Here again, objectivity is possible because of coordinating decentrations, which separate the invariables from the established functional variations.

The position in the sciences of man is far more complex, however, since a subject who observes or experiments on himself or others may not only be modified by the phenomena he observes, but may also generate modifications affecting the progress and even the nature of those phenomena. It is because of such situations that the fact of the observer being both object and subject creates additional difficulties in the case of the sciences of man by comparison with the natural sciences, in which the problem is generally that of dissociating subject and object. In other words, the centrifugal movement required to ensure objectivity is far harder to achieve where the object is composed of subjects. There are two reasons for this, both fairly systematic. The first is that the dividing line between the egocentric subject and the observed subject loses in definition as the observer's ego becomes involved in phenomena that he ought to be able to examine from a detached standpoint. The second reason is that the more "involved" the observer becomes and the more he attributes values to the facts he is studying, the more he is inclined to believe that he knows them intuitively and the less he feels a need for objective techniques.

Moreover, even though biology provides a series of transitional states between the behavior of elementary organisms and that of man, the latter exhibits various specific characteristics distinguished by the formation of collective cultures and the use of highly differentiated symptomatic or symbolic instruments (the "language" of bees being nothing more than a system of sensorimotor indices). Consequently, the object of the human sciences, which thus become a subject, differs fundamentally from the bodies and blind forces that constitute the object of the physical sciences, and even from the object-subjects of biological and ethological study. The difference, of course, is in the object's degree of consciousness, which is accentuated by the use of semiotic instruments. These, however, pose a further epistemological difficulty peculiar to the sciences of man: as means of communication, they often differ considerably from one human society to another; as a result, the psychologist or sociologist subject-observer is constantly obliged to verify whether his understanding is in fact "deep" enough for him to grasp the details of the symbolic structure of cultures remote from his own in space and time. He will even find himself asking whether man's psychophysiological characteristics may not be modified by a process of feedback from his semiotic instruments, and if so, to what extent. New disciplines such as A. Luria's neurolinguistics raise problems of this kind. In short, the central epistemological problem in the human sciences, namely, the individual being both subject and object, is aggravated by the fact that the object in turn is a conscious subject endowed with speech and multiple symbolisms; this makes objectivity and its prerequisites of decentration all the harder to achieve and often all the more limited.

II.

To begin with psychology, the various aspects of the circular relationship between the subject and the object and the difficulties of decentration find their *maximum* expression in the process of introspection—hence the variety of methods that have been adopted to overcome the basic obstacles either by going round them, at the risk of overlooking the essentials, or by treating them as problems in which the distortions caused by centration are studied as phenomenological indicators of the mechanisms of mental life itself.

In the pure form of introspection, a given individual is both an inquiring subject and the object of his inquiry. This being so, the subject is first of all modified by the object, and from two points of view: first, by his presuppositions about the value of introspection, in that this own mental life persuades him that he has an accurate vision of himself, whereas this vision in fact fulfills utilitarian rather than strictly cognitive or disinterested functions. From the cognitive point of view, it is centered on the external results of his action, and does not provide adequate information either about the mechanisms of that action or about the internal mechanisms of his mental life in general. From the affective point of view, the main function of this self-vision is to establish and maintain certain self-assigned values that help to maintain the subject's internal equilibrium rather than to enlighten us on the laws of that equilibrium. Second, the introspecting subject is modified by the object of his inquiry in that his entire activity, introspection included, is influenced to varying degrees by his past history, which is unknown to him because his memory of the past is the work of a very biased historian who forgets certain sources and distorts others, again as a result of arbitrary values that continually undermine the objectivity attributed by the subject both to his knowledge of the past and to his introspection in the present.

Conversely, introspection continually modifies the observed phenomena at every level. We know, for example, that periods of time are perceived as far longer if the subject tries to evaluate them while they are running their course. The role of mental images in thought used to give rise to all sorts of introspective errors until subjects were compared with one another and the difficulties of the problem realized. *A fortiori,* from the affective point of view, it is obvious that the introspection of feelings modifies them, either by giving them a cognitive dimension or by subordinating them to the values that, unknown to the subject, govern introspection itself. The reason why novelists and philosophers can use introspection successfully is precisely that their analysis is part of a certain vision of the world in which evaluation plays a central role. But where the problem is to investigate mechanisms as such, introspection is inadequate because it both modifies the observed phenomena and is distorted by them from the outset.

The immediate remedies (leaving aside for the time being all general methods and their various techniques) have been of three kinds. The first, of course, has been to decenter introspection itself by comparing the subjects with one another and confining the investigation to well-defined problems; the questions put to the subject then canalize the "simulated introspection" and allow systematic comparison to take place. This method has produced certain positive results, for example, as regards the dual nature of the judgment as an act and of the mental image. Chiefly, however, it has revealed the limits of introspection, whence Binet's disillusioned quip that "thought is an unconscious activity of the mind."

The second solution has been to eliminate introspection and study only behavior—a valuable step, since it paved the way for a far more fertile psychology of conduct than it was reasonable to expect. Many authors have found it too cramping, however, for two related reasons. The first is that unless we adopt Skinner's view that the organism is a "black box" described purely in terms of inputs and outputs, without any attempt at explanation, we are forced again and again to resort implicitly to introspective data; the "expectancy" that Tolman rightly stresses as a factor in all learning would remain incomprehensible unless we experienced it introspectively. The second reason is that problems are not solved merely by burying them; any psychology that ignores the conscious rules out the investigation of many facts whose interest lies precisely in their factuality. That these facts are "subjective" does not prevent the behaviorists from making implicit and frequent use of them, even if they are reluctant to recognize them among the objects of their investigations.

The third solution, on the other hand, is of great interest to the general epistemology of the sciences of man: it consists in acknowledging that introspection is deceptive, but then in asking why, and studying the cognitive distortions of the conscious, which are just as worthy of attention as any other phenomena in that they can be expected, under study, to reveal the laws that govern them and the factors that account for them. This, of course, within due limits, is a process of relativization similar to that of the physician, who instead of rejecting a time measurement made on our kinematic scale when he finds it cannot be applied to other cases, incorporates it in a system of covariations that gives it its limited significance (the error having merely consisted in regarding it as universal). With introspection, the situation is naturally far more complex, because the systematic and general errors due to the variable degrees or the shortcomings of decentered coordination (for example, recognizing only the results of operations and not seeing them as a constructive process, which is what happened to the Greeks in their mathematical thinking) are heightened by individual errors due to the multiplicity of egocentric approaches. Even these, however, obey laws, which it is not only interesting but also essential to elucidate.

Thus, from the affective point of view, the great merit of the psychoanalytic movements (even though their doctrines are not universally accepted down to the last detail) has been that instead of ignoring the conscious they have tried to work it into a dynamic system of larger dimensions explaining both the distortions to which the conscious is exposed and the limited but essential activities that characterize it (catharsis, for example, is not only a remedy for deviations caused by the unconscious, but also an appeal to conscious adjustment).

From the cognitive point of view, the psychology of "conduct," by contrast with that of mere behavior, restores the conscious to its functional aspect; this explains both its adaptive role as well as its shortcomings and errors. Claparède, for example, used the term "the law of *prise de conscience*" to describe the process whereby the conscious concentrates on zones of action in which inadaptation is a fact or a possibility and ignores mechanisms that function of their own accord without need of supervision. Hence the fact that the conscious proceeds from the periphery toward the central processes (cf. consciousness of the results of operations preceding recognition of their constructive significance) instead of focusing on the inner life, as introspection naïvely imagines, and thence acting centrifugally. The psychology of conduct also accounts for time illusions—which remain unexplained as the mere intuition of the period elapsed—by restoring the perception of time to a context of kinematic adjustments of action, and so forth. In short, in many fields, the facts of consciousness, the capacity for distortion and the efficiency of which are both so puzzling, yield an interpretation immediately as the distortion becomes a problem in itself and the facts requiring explanation can be seen in a decentered context. As we shall see in Section v, it is this approach that enables the psychological subject to dissociate himself from the human subject that he is investigating as an object (it remains to be seen how he is able to do so).

III.

Sociology poses an even more acute epistemological problem than psychology, because its object is not merely an individual subject that is external, although analogous, to the psychological subject, but also a collective "we" that is all the more difficult to identify objectively because the sociological subject forms part of it, either directly or indirectly (in this case through other similar or rival communities). In such a situation, the sociologist himself is constantly modified by the object of his research; this is so from birth onward, since he is the product of a continuous educative and social process. Far from being an intellectual conjecture, we can point to precise examples. For instance, we know that the many political comments with which Pareto embellished his famous *Tratto di sociologia generale,* and which he somewhat ingenuously regarded as evidence of his scientific objectivity, were due to an attitude acquired from reacting against a father of progressive convictions. We have here an example both of the difficulty of avoiding ideological influences when dealing with sociology, and of a conflict between generations that is not only Freudian but also related to certain social environments concerned with ideas as much as with affective problems.

Conversely, the sociologist modifies the facts he observes. It is not that he behaves like the psychologist, who experiments in ways that put the subject in positions unfamiliar to him and thereby partly transform his behavior—one cannot experiment on society as a whole. But precisely insofar as sociology aims at grasping that whole and goes beyond microsociological analyses of particular relationships, such a problem—and this is true of microsociological research itself—can only be solved by reference to theoretical or operational concepts, either metasociological or concerned with the facts as such, which involve a certain carving up of reality and in particular an active structuration on the part of the investigator. This structuration naturally forces the facts into molds—molds either made for the purpose or borrowed from other disciplines, but with a very variable capacity for objectivization, i.e., for faithfully reflecting the structures of reality or, on the other hand, for distortion or involuntary selection. Let us remember, however, and this will recall that the epistemological problem of sociology is far from insoluble, that this active structuration of reality is inherent in all experimental research, physical, biological, or sociological, since however accurately experience may be interpreted, the process cannot take place outside a logico-mathematical framework; the richer the framework, the more objective the interpretation. Thus a simple act like reading a temperature on a thermometer involves not only the movements of the mercury up and down the tube, which are independent of the subject (despite the fact that he has selected this phenomenon as significant and built the apparatus), but also a whole system of measurements calling for logical categories, order, number, the division of spatial continuity, the grouping of movements, the choice of a unit, and so on. But the framework with which the subject thus enriches the object, far from distorting it, forms a structure of functional relations that enable him to identify the objective processes he is seeking to discover. In the case of society as a whole, however, the problem is far more complex, because the whole is not perceptible; the choice of the variables or indicators used to portray and analyze it will therefore depend on far more complex intellectual activities on the part of the sociological subject than with a physical measurement. These activities will therefore be less quantifiable as regards their capacity for objectivization or, alternatively, for distortion or error.

In fact, there are only three major types of possible structurations of the whole,[7] with many subvarieties. That this is true in all fields clearly demonstrates the existence of the factors of unconscious decision and objectivizating, or conversely, of distorting the assimilation of reality. This leads us to assert that when a sociologist observes facts he always modifies them, either by enriching, but not falsifying them—i.e., by using frameworks that merely reproduce the objective links and make them conceptually acceptable—or by forcing them into structures that ignore the essentials or more or less systematically distort them. The three major types of structuration are additive or atomistic composition, in which society is conceived as a sum of individuals already possessing the characteristics requiring explanation; emergence, in which the whole as such generates new properties that are imposed on the individuals; and relational totality, a system of interactions that modify the individuals from the outset and also explain variations in the whole.[8] Depending on the

---

[7] See *Main Trends in Interdisciplinary Research*, section 5.

[8] An example will illustrate the difference between the second and third types. Durkheim (emergence) sees the obligation imposed by the conscience as a product of the constraint exercised by society as a whole on individuals, including parents, whose authority over their children is respected only in so far as it emanates from the collective law (cf. respect in Kant). J. M. Baldwin, P. Bovet and Freud, on the other hand, maintain that respect is explained by the affective relationship between

choice of model—a choice dictated, both involuntarily and consciously, by general theoretical considerations and not only by the subject's education, which may be individualistic, authoritarian, or other, according to his social group—the facts observed are bound to be modified immediately as they are selected and throughout the structuration process, from identification to interpretation. Consequently what Tarde takes as imitation is regarded by Durkheim as a formative constraint, by Pareto as an expression of hereditary instincts, and so on; what the idealist sees as the products of widely held group "doctrines" are regarded by the Marxist as deep-seated conflicts, of which the doctrines are merely a symbolic reflection and an ideological compensation, and so forth.

Nevertheless, just as introspective illusions obviously raise a problem of fact, which as such concerns psychology, so the modifications induced in the sociologist's mind by the society that has shaped him, and the modifications induced in the social material by the mind of the sociologist, whose task is to structuralize that material, are social facts of interest to sociology insofar as it is able to study them. Although the epistemological problem is therefore even more complicated in sociology than in psychology, there is nothing insoluble about it. Section v will deal with the various kinds of intellectual decentering that can be used to solve it.

IV.

Economics suffers from the same difficulties. As evidence of this, we need only consider the extent to which Marxism regarded the classical economy as reflecting an ideology based on class. Consequently, however accurately an economic law reflects the observed facts, there are always grounds for questioning just how general it is, in view of its dependence on a relatively special structure that the economist, if trained in it and conceiving it through insufficiently decentered models, is inclined to regard as general. Fernand Braudel, in maintaining that economics is a question of "all structures and all conjunctures, and not only of material infrastructures and infracon-

---

parents and children, which makes the parents' examples or instructions coercive, the moral constraints of the group as a whole being built up from such interactions.

junctures"—of "social structures and conjunctures" up to the level of "civilization"—shows that although metrical and statistical data are far easier to come by in economics than in sociology, the principle underlying the epistemological problem of deciphering experience objectively, and of interpreting it, is just as complex in the former discipline as in the latter.

Ethnology, on the other hand, has the great advantage of dealing with societies of which the observer is not an integral part. But the question remains of determining what the observer, when faced with data external to himself, has injected in the form of conceptual instruments in order to be able to structuralize them. Even if we knew nothing of the philosophical molding or intellectual habits of such men as Frazer, Lévy-Bruhl, and Lévi-Strauss, it would not be altogether impossible to reconstruct them by studying what these writers had to say on myth or on the mode of reasoning of the subjects of their inquiries. The question then is whether Frazer's laws of the association of ideas, the logical relativism of Lévy-Bruhl, and the structuralism of Lévi-Strauss are nearer the subjects' minds or the authors'. Structuralism can immediately be seen to fit the facts better than the other two approaches (and what is more, without conflicting with a constructivist view that embodies the essence of Lévy-Bruhl's "prelogic" provided we put aside his radical heterogeneities, global "mentalities," and so on, concepts that ignore the techniques). But this is not because structuralism confines itself to copying the observed data; on the contrary, it integrates the facts into algebraico-logical systems that reproduce their shape without distortion and render them acceptable to general modes of explanation.

In linguistics, the modification of the observer by the facts he observes is less marked, since a linguist, by profession, is a comparatist who does not reduce everything to his own language and concerns himself with the differences no less than with the similarities between the languages he is comparing. But once again, this does not mean that the theory is merely a structure matching the facts to be interpreted, because the further linguistic structuralism progresses, the more firmly committed it becomes to the technique of abstract models, which enrich the linguistic material with logico-mathematical structures.

Lastly, we have demography, which poses fewer of the specifically human science problems of subject-object relationship than any of our other disciplines. This is because it deals with more easily quantifiable data and thus involves fewer of those circular or dialectical situations that, although a source of difficulty, contribute to the particular richness of the sciences of man.[9]

The difficulties outlined above may seem insurmountable, but a comparison between the beginnings of scientific psychology—a discipline in which those difficulties are especially prominent—and the flourishing science it has now become is nothing if not reassuring. One is left wondering at the hidden means whereby these problems, even if not fully solved, have at least been divested of their mystery.

V.

These means, although fairly simple in principle, become increasingly complex in practice as experimentation augments in difficulty. A situation in which the subject of a mode of acquiring knowledge is modified by the object of his study and in turn modifies it, constitutes the prototype of a dialectical interaction. There are two principal methods of approaching such interactions, and it is precisely these two kinds of method that are normally described in dialectical terms as well. On the one hand, the task is to clarify such interactions in terms of their development, in other words to set them in a historical or genetic context; on the other, it is to analyze them in terms of disequilibria and restored equilibria, in other words, of auto-adjustments and causal interactional circuits.

In the field of psychology, for example, the most effective method of dissociation in an interpretation, or even in a descriptive analysis of facts concerning adult behavior or consciousness, is to trace it to its source in infancy. There are two reasons for this. The first is that the only way to obtain a causal explanation of a system of reactions is to study the way in which it was formed, since a structure is only comprehensible through an understanding of its composition. Even in the case of adjustments whose driving power is synchronistic, we still need to know how they have come about; here again, the study of the process becomes explanatory. The second reason is that inso-

[9] Except in areas such as migration and urbanization, where demography and sociology are probably bound to interact.

far as a structure attributed to an adult individual can be suspected of belonging more to the observer than to the subject of his observation, a study of the various stages of its development furnishes a body of objective references that is difficult to mold deliberately in order to fit subjective theories. In other words, if the suspect structure exists only in the mind of the theorist, it is impossible to detect traces of its formation in the subjects at previous stages, whereas if the formative process can be followed step by step, there is no longer any reason for doubting the objective existence of its final outcome.[10]

The other method of ascertaining that this function is, in fact, being performed by a structure in the mind of the subject, and that the structure itself is not merely a product of the observer's own process of conceptualization, consists in studying its effect on the subject's pattern of behavior or of thought. For example, children aged seven to eight are believed to be capable of building mental structures of the type $A < B < C \ldots$, which are put together by a process of trial and error. Given that logic characterizes such sequences as interconnected and transitive series of asymmetrical relations, it suffices to examine whether subjects capable of building them are also able to proceed further and, without seeing X and Z together, but knowing merely that $X < Y$ and $Y < Z$, to arrive at the completely new conclusion that $X < Z$. This is in fact what is observed, although it was not at all apparent before.

In sociological fields, where experimentation is well-nigh impossible, the historical or sociogenetic method is of fundamental importance in enabling the observer to understand in what social cur-

[10] For example, we have come to believe that the "natural logic" of the adolescent and the adult represents a "group" structure of four transformations in which an inverse transformation, a reciprocal, a correlative and an identical correspond to each propositional operation (e.g., an implication). This leads us to ask whether such a Klein group really exists in the subject's intellectual behavior (not in his deliberate consciousness, of course, but in his modes of reasoning), or whether the psychologist has simply translated the facts into this convenient language while wrongly projecting such a structure into the minds of his subjects. However, since it is easy to demonstrate the formation between seven and twelve years of age of structures based on operations whose form of reversibility is inversion (such as the classification $+A - A = 0$) or reciprocity ($A = B$, so $B = A$), it is highly likely that the two kinds of systems, when translated into terms of propositions, will finally combine to produce a synthesis including both forms of reversibility, whence the group in question.

rents he himself is being borne along. When, on the other hand, he is involved both as judge and participant in contemporary crises or conflicts, a detailed analysis of the forms of social causality nevertheless allows the observer to achieve a degree of decentering, limited as it may be, by revealing that what he is inclined to consider as one-way causal liaisons are always circular liaisons with reverse actions. In such a case, it is impossible to pursue the analysis without coming to the conclusion that with society, as with individuals, there are at least two levels of behavior: actual behavior, and a state of awareness not always matching that behavior; in other words, there are substructures that are accessible to truly causal research, and conceptual or ideological systems by which individuals in a society justify and explain to themselves their social behavior. All sociologists, in fact, conduct such research and make such distinctions, and are able in consequence to arrive at a state of decentered objectivity. But although the latter makes it possible to dissociate the patterns conceived by the observer from the facts that he observes, it will always be incomplete and subject to revision, since the patterns themselves remain subject to ideological influences. Some sociologists conclude from this that scientific objectivity, as understood in the natural sciences, is unattainable in sociology and that cognitive progress in this field is only possible if research is associated with the commitment of the observer to a specific praxis; but the very wish to take systematic account of this conclusion constitutes in this respect a means of distinguishing between the subject and the object of research, since even in physics, objectivity does not lie in alienation or separation from a phenomenon, but rather in acting upon an object in such a way as to provoke a phenomenon: what is "observable" is never more than the product of the impact of experiment upon reality. There is this difference, however: that the phenomena observed in physics may be more easily measured and coordinated in logico-mathematical structures than may social phenomena, which are far more global. But if then a distinction is made in sociology between relations that are measurable and what is sometimes called the "metasociological" zone, because it can only be reached through theoretical speculation, there are grounds for hoping that the shifting frontier between these areas may be gradually pushed back.

Similar problems exist in economics, but here, since measurement is always easier and mathematical or econometric theory far more advanced, the problem is reduced to one of adjusting theoretical models to experimental patterns (in the broadest sense of the term). This brings us to the next series of questions.

4

Experimental Methods and the Analysis of Factual Data

The epistemological difficulties encountered in the human sciences, of which we have just given an outline, naturally center upon questions of method, since the most outstanding result of interactions between subject and object in the disciplines with which we are here concerned is to tender experimentation, in the sense in which it is practiced in the natural sciences, particularly difficult.

In psychology, which deals with the behavior of individuals external to the observer himself, experimentation is, in principle, neither more nor less complex than in biology; the main difference lies in the fact that human beings cannot be subjected to whatever experiment seems opportune, and that in contrast to physiology, animals cannot in these particular cases be substituted for humans. On the other hand, whenever collective phenomena are involved, as in sociology, economics, linguistics, or demography, experimentation in the strict sense (i.e., the modification of phenomena through the free variation of factors) is obviously impossible and can only be replaced by systematic observation based on factual variations and the analysis of those variations in a functional—i.e., logical and mathematical—fashion.

I.

Before, however, going into these situations in detail, it would be appropriate to recall that these particular difficulties with regard to experimentation are not peculiar to the human sciences, nor are they all due to the fact that what is under examination is a collectivity of which the observer is or may be a member. The prime difficulty is of a far more general order, and derives from the impossibility of acting at will upon the objects of observation when the latter are on a higher than individual scale: this difficulty in connection with the scale of phenomena is not, however, peculiar to the social sciences, and may be found in such natural sciences as astronomy and particularly cosmology and geology, which are historical disciplines as well.

The case of astronomy is doubly interesting. In the first place, it shows that a high degree of precision is possible without experimentation on the scale of the object under study, through a convergence of theoretical patterns and actual measurements, provided the latter are sufficiently numerous and exact. Thus, for example, Newton's system of celestial mechanics produced a most remarkable correspondence, of the order of a fraction of a second, between theory and the metrical measurements, with a single minute divergence concerning the perihelion of Mercury. Such convergences make it possible to organize the equivalent of experiments concerning a hitherto unexamined problem, in which measurements are compared with novel theoretical conclusions; one such "experiment" was that conducted by Michelson and Morley, when they measured the velocity of light in terms of a moving source and a moving observer. Their measurements having shown that these mobilities were without effect, they were faced with a choice among three conclusions: that the measurements were open to doubt (they were, in fact, proved to be accurate); that the general principle of relativity was erroneous (a conclusion that had been rationally unacceptable from the time of Galileo); or that space and time were relative to velocity—a conclusion adopted in relativistic mechanics, which also permitted a satisfactory approximation to the perihelion of Mercury.

Hence we see that the concordance between calculation and measurement does in fact lead to the equivalent of experiment where the organization of the measurements can be based upon reasonable forecasts, i.e., in situations where observation makes it possible to choose between precise alternative paths. But there is a further indirect manner in which experimentation can always take place: from a general theory concerning phenomena the scale of which makes the dissociation of factors impossible, one may sometimes draw conclusions on a scale that lends itself to experimental action. In such cases, control experiments are possible, as, for example, when Newtonian mechanics was applied in the laboratory (in the measurement of weight, etc.), or when the theory of relativity gave rise to a number of equally verifiable conclusions (experiments by Ch. E. Guye and Lavanchy concerning the relationship between mass and energy, and so on).

We may note here that successes of this type in astronomy, despite the impossibility of conducting large-scale experiments, give rise to hope in the case of such disciplines as econometrics or even sociology, provided measurements are precise enough to permit adequate comparison with theoretical patterns. But a further major difficulty to be added to that of measurement arises from the fact that social phenomena all depend to a greater or less extent on the unfolding of history, and that such diachronic processes do not lend themselves either to experimentation or even to the elaboration of properly deductive patterns. Here again, however, the situation is not peculiar to the human sciences; geology, for example, lends itself neither to experimentation nor to deduction in the strict sense.

In geology, nevertheless, once the strata providing the necessary chronological framework have been established (on the basis of stratigraphy supported by mineralogical and paleontological data), it is possible to elaborate what are, in fact, causal series, such as those embodied in the general tectonic theories of Termier concerning overthrust, of Wegener concerning the movement of continents, and of Argand concerning the formation of Alpine chains through successive earth movements. Such geological laws are based on certain historically regular processes, but they also conform to certain structural laws. For example, the mathematician Wavre drew up equations concerning the effects of the rotation of more or less fluid masses, in a structural analysis that, *inter alia,* provided support for Wegener's formulations.

As regards the natural sciences in the context of historical processes that can no longer be challenged but on which some light can still be shed by modern experimentation—as, for example, when the theory of the evolution of organized beings is set against genetics—it goes without saying that they are, in principle, better placed, because they draw at one and the same time on data provided by experiments, however limited, and on mathematical patterns (great services have already been rendered in genetics by the elaboration of mathematical models of processes of selection and reassembly). Yet the complexity of the problems involved and the impossibility of large-scale experimentation place these disciplines in a position somewhat similar to that occupied by the social sciences, so that, in the last analysis, the sciences of man cannot be systematically and from the outset relegated to a position of inferiority.

II.

It remains nevertheless that the methodological problems encountered in experimentation, measurement, and the confrontation of data provided by experiment with theoretical patterns are a source of particular difficulty as far as the sciences of man are concerned. These problems are not, as we have just seen, to any great extent due to the limited possibilities of experimentation, a difficulty also encountered in certain of the natural sciences on grounds of scale or of historical development; in principle, experimentation in the strict sense of the term may, as we have seen, be replaced by adequate analysis of the data provided by observation and measurement. The most serious problem—and here the obstacles encountered by the sciences of man are comparable with those met with in a number of biological disciplines—is that of measurement itself, i.e., the degree of precision with which the facts determined by observation can be noted.

Measurement consists, in principle, in applying number to the discontinuous or continuous data that are to be evaluated. And if recourse is had to number, this is not because of the prestige of mathematics or because of some prejudice in favor of quantity, for quantity is merely a relationship between qualities and it is impossible to dissociate the qualitative and quantitative aspects of any structure, even one that is purely logical.[11] The instrumental value of number derives from the fact that it constitutes a structure that is far richer than that of its logical components: class—which is predominant in

---

[11] It is the qualitative aspects of purely mathematical structures which preoccupy mathematicians; to identify mathematics with the study of quantity would be grossly to ignore the significance of modern work in this field.

systems of classification; and order—which is the chief characteristic of seriations. As a synthesis of class and order, number thus offers an abundance and a mobility that make its structures particularly useful in all matters related to comparison, i.e., correspondences and isomorphisms; hence the necessity of measurement.

But the use of measurement and the application of number presuppose the creation of "unities," that is, the casting aside of qualitative differences between a number of elements in favor of what they have in common. Until a system of unities has been organized, structural analysis may only be attempted along the two complementary lines of interlocking or ordinal systems, which furnish more or less complete substitutes or more or less approximative measurements, but fall short of exact measurement. Exact measurement only becomes possible, in fact, in physics, chemistry, astronomy, and so forth, when systems of unities have been constituted whose intrinsic properties and whose relationships are such that it is possible to pass from one unity to another.

The chief difficulty with the sciences of man, and indeed with all the life sciences, as soon as group structures and not merely isolated and particular processes are involved, lies in the absence of unities of measurement, either because it has not yet proved possible to constitute such unities, or because the structures in question, although quite possibly of a logico-mathematical nature (algebraic, ordinal, topological, probabilistic, and so on), do not present specifically numerical characteristics.

A. Of all the sciences of man, the only one that is not affected by this fundamental difficulty is demography, in which the yardstick is the number of individuals possessing a given characteristic. But it is precisely because, in such cases, the statistical methods utilized may be kept relatively simple (despite the complexity of certain problems of growth), that such methods cannot be applied without further ado to other sectors of the human sciences. Consequently demographic studies, although of basic importance to economic and sociological research, remain relatively hermetic,[12] although fruitful, the

[12] "Relatively," in comparison with the other sciences of man, although a number of problems are obviously common to sociology and demography, and the subject of essentially interdisciplinary research, migration and urbanization being particularly striking examples.

impossibility of experimentation (in the strict sense of dissociation of
factors) being compensated for by the relative precision of measurements and the success of the different statistical methods applied to
variations and to the different functional relationships open to
calculation.

B. Scientific psychology is, in some respects, diametrically opposed
to demography, in the double sense that although experimentation is
relatively simple, there is an almost total lack of unities in which
formative or functional processes themselves may be measured. Experimentation is, as we have stated, of the same type in biology as in
psychology, since it concerns behavior, which is one aspect of life in
general. It is relatively feasible in certain cases to bring about variation in a single factor or a single group of factors, the others being
more or less neutralized; the difficulty here is to maintain a situation of "all other things being equal," since organisms, like behavior,
are functional entities whose elements are more or less interdepen-
dent. In the case of human behavior, the impossibility, on occasion,
of dissociating factors is due as much to moral as to technical considerations; but pathological states frequently provide the experimenter with what he cannot obtain through actual experimentation:
for example, aphasia and deaf-mutism are, in fact, the expression of
a dissociation between language and thought. Moreover, if the human subject is less amenable to manipulation than the animal, he
does have the great advantage of being able, as a general rule, to
describe verbally a part of his own reactions. As far as the historical
or diachronic dimensions of psychology are concerned, if the paleontology and prehistory of man provide virtually no information regarding mentality (unless we follow Leroi-Gourhan's example in
seeking to reconstitute intelligence through the study of techniques),
the psychology of individual development can make use of experimentation at all age levels, and is thus an inexhaustible mine of
knowledge concerning formative mechanisms.

On the other hand the main difficulty in psychology lies in the
lack of unities of measurement. It is true that the "test" method,
together with countless "psychophysical" procedures, provides a
wealth of data that are termed metric because they are solely concerned with aspects of behavior that can be measured, i.e., with the

resultants of reactions or, as some would say, with "performance." But, even if we confine ourselves to such resultants, we are still unable to talk of unities of measurement: if, for example, a subject retains 8 words out of 15 in a memory test, or 4 out of 6 sectors of a spatial journey, we have no means of knowing whether these words or sectors are equivalent as between each other, nor do we know how to compare the memory of words with that of a journey.[13] What is more—much more—the measurement of a resultant tells us nothing yet about the inner mechanisms of the observed reaction, and it is precisely those mechanisms that should be measured. It is, of course, possible to arrive—through a system of correlation raised to the second power—at a so-called factorial analysis, but we know neither the nature of the "factors" thus disclosed nor their mode of action, so that they remain in fact entirely related to the tests utilized, and thus to the resultants or performances, and bear no direct relationship to the formative mechanisms. Briefly, then, the metrical procedures of psychology do provide data that are useful in the step-by-step comparison of details concerning the results of various mental operations, but because of the absence of any system of units permitting the passage from effects back to the causal mechanism, those operations remain inaccessible.

But the situation is by no means hopeless, or even disquieting, for there are other logico-mathematical structures besides those that are numerical or metric, and while number may be a particularly practical tool in processes of comparison, there are many other forms of isomorphism besides numerical correspondence. The difficulty in creating systems of units may thus spring from the nature of the biological, mental, or biological-mental structures themselves, in which case such structures might lend themselves to topological or qualitative algebraic treatment rather than to processes involving numerical "groups," "rings," or "bodies." Philosophers have often speculated on this resistance to measurement in psychology. Psychologists, more prudently, in the first place refuse to consider the

[13] Let us suppose that in an examination a candidate receives 12 marks out of 20 in mathematics and 10 out of 20 in history: there is no means of determining whether the difference between 11 and 12 is the same as that between 9 and 10, or between 2 and 3; nor whether these wholly symbolic numbers are comparable in the two branches in question.

matter as settled, and in the meantime make use of broader and more flexible logico-mathematical instruments and structures, ranging from one extreme (the many probabilistic models) to the other (the models of algebraic logic) without, of course, neglecting cybernetic models. Thus, in the sphere of intelligence, qualitative algebraic structures permit the description of operations themselves and not merely of their products and resultants—which are all that can be measured at the present time. Moreover, these operations may be analyzed as perfectly balanced products of numerous genetically anterior determinations that then derive from cybernetic models (including those related to the theory of decisions or the theory of games). In all questions of development, where measurement, properly speaking, is of no assistance, at least at the present time, it is still possible to turn for assistance to scales of hierarchic ordination (such as those of Guttman); and Suppes has described a whole range of scales between nominal and metrical classification: mention may be made in particular of "hyperordinal" scales, where intervals between one value and the next cannot be reduced to unitary factors (equivalent between themselves), but may already be evaluated as greater or lesser than one another.

Thanks to these different models, psychology, even though it has not yet overcome the problem of measurement in the sense of an absolute reduction to number and to unit systems, is in possession of statistical data and of qualitative logico-mathematical structures that are sufficient to permit, in many cases, a certain degree of prediction of phenomena (for example in the fields of perception and intelligence) and in particular the beginning of some form of explanation (see Chapter 7).

C. Economics is roughly halfway between the extremes of demography and psychology: measurement is easier than it is in psychology, but experimentation is less easy, the difficulties being comparable to those encountered in demography. However, some of the many attempts of states or private enterprise to manipulate the economy can be regarded as experiments (conducted with varying degrees of success).

Measurements are more feasible in economics than in psychology, for it is in the nature of exchanges of values occurring in such a field to be quantified, as opposed to the qualitative exchanges that generally characterize social relations of a moral, political, or affective type. For instance, if two students enjoy seeing each other, or find it interesting, one to discuss mathematics, the other linguistics, this cannot be called an economic exchange; but if they agree to put this exchange on a regular footing and set one hour for mathematics in exchange for one for linguistics, the arrangement becomes economic, even though the contents of the exchange are the same as before, and measurement is involved (at least a measure of time, failing one of information or ideas supplied). Prices, currency, and so forth, thus constitute a set of quantifications that are not just ordinal or "intensive,"[14] but extensive or metric. In the various branches of economics it is therefore easy to find occasion for much authentic measurement using units peculiar to this or that sector (for example, output per inhabitant in the comparison of socioeconomic aggregates). But we are still a long way from a complete system of units capable of being equated, as in physics.

On the other hand, in economics, experimentation is not feasible in the strict sense of assigning and systematically varying the factors. It can here be broadly defined as "any direct or indirect action brought to bear on a given situation for the purpose of producing or obtaining observable consequences" (Solari). Actually, experimentation at this level consists mainly in observation governed by a system of abstractions, in turn inspired by the theoretical models adopted as hypotheses. It is therefore the combination of the theoretical model and the experimental pattern, i.e., a pattern laying down what is to be observed and what procedure is to be followed, that constitutes the basic methodological approach in econometrics. In this interaction between the deductive and the experimental process, as also in the role played by methodical abstraction, the general character of all the sciences, natural and human, is immediately recognizable.

The real difficulty with this discipline, given the lack of experi-

---

[14] If A is included in B in the form $A + A' = B$, intensive quality is involved as we only know that $A < B$ without knowing the relationship between A and A'. Extensive quantity is involved when we do know these relationships (for example, $A < A'$), and metric quantity appears with the introduction of units (for example $B = 2A$ because $A = A'$).

mentation in the strict sense and the fact that synchronic and diachronic factors are ever-present and extraordinarily complex, is how
to adjust the theoretical model to the experimental patterns, for the
latter are likely to be so global and insufficiently differentiated as to
rule out an analysis leading to decisions. As a theoretical model does
not lead to a practical interpretation that can actually be verified, it
is only a logical pattern. Conversely, a set of observations that is not
rather fully structured is merely descriptive.

Now the theoretical models used in economics are becoming more
and more highly refined: mathematical logic, mechanical and sto-
chastic models, the theory of games and operational methods (with
linear and nonlinear programs), cybernetic models, and so on, are
used either singly or together, with historical analyses and analyses
of institutional parameters where necessary. Then again the application of all these methods to experimental data is constantly im-
peded by the difficulty of delimiting the fields of observation, hence
of finding the opportune level of abstraction, for alongside general
laws and laws that are not general but apply to more than one economic aggregate, there are laws peculiar to a single aggregate, and
problems of typology are continually arising according to the scale
of values adopted.

D. Linguistics provides an excellent example of a science in which
experimentation is almost excluded (except in experimental pho-
netics and psycholinguistics) and in which systematic analysis of
observable data has proved sufficient to permit the establishment of
methods, the exactness of which could serve as an example in other
human sciences. Yet in this field also, as in psychology, attempts to
work out systems of units of measurement have been unsuccessful,
except in particular or, so to speak, localized cases in which the units
are selected arbitrarily in a restricted context.

The search for regularities (linguists refer less and less to "laws,"
not wishing to conjure up an illusory similarity with the laws of
physics) is based essentially on the model of the logical functions,
particularly that of implication. We know that the expression "x implies y" means that we observe y whenever x is given, that y can be
observed without x, that neither x nor y may be observable, but that
we never have x without y. In phonology, for example, we note that

p and *b* are both explosive phonemes, but that only the latter requires the use of the vocal cords, and that this situation allows us to expect certain regularities in their common functioning and their contrasts.

But starting from such regularities of logical and qualitative form, we can naturally follow two opposite though complementary paths: that of statistical regularities in the external resultants of the functioning of language, and that of analysis of the internal structures whose functioning is their expression. As an example of the first tendency, we might quote Zipf's "law," stating a more or less regular relationship between species and *genera* in verbal classifications. The probabilist nature of such statements leads us to the problem of their explanation in terms of the objects designated, the subject of the language, or both. On the diachronic level (and in its connections with synchronic balance), Martinet has attempted to explain phonological changes as a compromise between the need to express oneself and the tendency toward economy, of psychological or probabilist origin. The role of entropy in communication theory is known: Whatnough has quite recently used it for linguistic purposes.

All the research in structural linguistics, such as that by Chomsky, can be quoted to illustrate the second tendency, one of the aims of which is to discover regularities in the very transformations of possible rules while still leaving open the question of explanatory models, sought, by Saumjan and others, in the direction of cybernetic structures.

In short, we can see here how a human science, though lacking almost all means of experimentation and all recourse to units of measurement of a general character, manages on the double plane of diachronic successions and of synchronic regulations to build up a methodology exact enough to allow of constant and often exemplary progress.

E. Sociology and ethnology doubtless occupy the most difficult position among all the human sciences, for three reasons: the impossibility of conducting experiments, the lack of general units of measurement, and the complexity of the phenomena, which depend upon all the factors affecting human life and behavior (unlike a relatively well-defined field of research such as that of linguistics).

To revert to the comparison with the natural sciences referred to in Section I, sociology resembles astronomy as regards the impossibility of experimentation, but without the benefit of measurements converging with mathematical deduction; and it resembles geology as regards the predominance of nondeductible diachronic and qualitative factors, but without the advantage of an adequate stratigraphy or paleontology.

Five methods can be followed, however, in order to meet this lacunary situation. The first naturally consists in refining the mathematical analysis of functional relationships and subsummations. A series of advances has recently been made in this connection, particularly by the use of what is known as multivariate analysis, which allows of going beyond correlations and seeking causes. The "Columbia School" has produced in this way much research on public opinion (see in particular P. F. Lazarsfeld's work on two-step flow, which brings out the factors of interest, passivity, or plasticity, the mechanisms at work in opinion manipulation, and so forth).

The second method consists in seeking, behind the observable data, the role of the "structures" as systems of transformation whose mobile equilibrium lends itself to analysis by qualitative mathematics (general algebra). This is the structuralist method used by Claude Lévi-Strauss, which tends to go beyond causality as a functional relationship between observable data and to seek explanation, resting on both causes and implications, that account for the same data in terms of the underlying overall systems.

The third method, chiefly evident in schools that have been subjected to Marxist influences, consists in coordinating structuralist and historical analysis, the explanation being then obtained by combining structure and genesis. Along with ethnological research (and we must note here that for some years there has been renewed interest throughout the world in the political and cultural aspects of development), these historicostructuralist trends are of course likely to make for the decentering of Western observers.

A fourth method (touched upon by analogy in our brief remarks about astronomy) consists in studying, on a lower level, the repercussions or parallels of the major phenomena on the higher level. This is the task of microsociology, and it has yielded significant findings through experiments on the dynamics of small groups and analyses of elementary social behavior patterns. But the problems to which this method constantly gives rise are those of bridging the gaps between the various levels, for the central problem of sociology is still that of the relationship between subsystems, or between them and the overall system. Tentative theoretical answers have been of two kinds. Some have taken the form of fairly systematic attempts at building up abstract models (in the language of logico-mathematical symbolism, but sometimes also by methods of simulation). Others amount to combining structuralism with functionalist analysis within the detailed field of social relations or actions. Thus T. Parsons' general sociology, which he himself calls "structural-functional," is concerned not only with types of overall balance of society, but also with reconciling levels by means of an analysis of elementary "social action" (values, and so forth). Similarly A. W. Gouldner's or P. M. Blau's "neofunctionalism" seeks, through the study of "reciprocities" and exchanges, a tool for coordinating subsystems that will lead from interindividual relations to the stratifications themselves.

The fifth method has been little used, but remains open in the eyes of many authors: since the training of the rising generation by its predecessors is a necessary (although not sufficient) condition of all social life, any comparative study of the development of human beings in various social environments provides decisive information concerning collective contributions to human nature. On every question that arises—social, mental, or biological character, logic, moral sentiments, semiotic or symbolic systems, and so on—this method of analyzing the formative processes is undoubtedly rewarding, and has already revealed the deep natural identity of the "operations" of individual thought with those that occur in any social "cooperation."

5

The Sciences of Man and the
Great Philosophical or Ideological Trends

After reviewing some aspects of the sciences of man and the main difficulties encountered in their definition and development, the moment would appear to have come to fit them into the general system of sciences as suggested in the title of this essay. But to all the previously mentioned obstacles that have to be surmounted if we are to reach an objective understanding of human realities, there must be added yet another, perhaps one of the most important and in any case the most specific in terms of the differences between the sciences of man and those of nature. It is therefore necessary to deal with this now, before we compare the two groups within the complete system of scientific disciplines.

This overriding difficulty, closely connected with those of intellectual decentering that have already been discussed in Chapter 2 and the hold of the *"we"* over the cognitive matter that creates a science (see Chapter 3), simply derives from the fact that a scientist is never completely objective but is always at the same time committed to some philosophical or ideological attitude. This point is only of secondary importance in mathematical, physical, or even biological research (we already reach a frontier region in the latter case), but it may have a great influence in some of the problems dealt with in the sciences of man. Linguistics is approximately the same thing in every country. Psychology varies somewhat more according to the cultural environment, but with no disturbing contradictions, as the variations in question depend more on the variety of schools than on ideologies. The oppositions become sharper in economics and especially in sociology. Broadly speaking then, we are faced with a problem that we should now consider.

More exactly, there are several kinds of problems, depending on whether the ideological or philosophical currents support some one or other particular trend in research, whether they are likely to conceal some aspect or other of the field to be investigated, or whether they may eventually atrophy some discipline or other by implicit or even explicit opposition to its development. The method to be followed is therefore that of selecting some particular examples and drawing conclusions limited to each of them individually.

I.

An initial, somewhat striking example is that of empirical philosophy, which has a very lasting tradition in Anglo-Saxon ideologies, one of the present-day sequels being the movement known as "logical empiricism" or "positivism." This empirical philosophy has in fact played a not insignificant part in the formation and development of certain aspects of the sciences of man, though imposing on them at the same time certain orientations that other schools today find rather restrictive.

One may certainly say in favor of empirical philosophy that it has been one of the sources of psychology and scientific sociology, in the sense that it anticipated the future need for them and even contributed to their development. Locke sought to resolve problems by basing himself on facts and not on mere speculation, while Hume put as the subtitle of his famous treatise "An Attempt to Introduce the Experimental Method of Reasoning into Moral Subjects." The whole of Anglo-Saxon psychology was initially soaked in this kind of atmosphere, and the "English anthropological school," with Tylor, Frazer, and many others, was also inspired by it. One cannot therefore deny that an ideological current of this kind contributed positively to the advancement of the sciences of man; nor ought we to neglect the contemporary contributions of logical empiricism to the development of logic and of the theory of sciences.

But precisely as a philosophy or the crystallization of an ideology, empiricism (obviously a very general term that by no means excludes

countless individual variants) in some cases has also played a direc-
tional or canalizing role that psychologists, sociologists, and non-
empiricist logicians could regard as restrictive. For empiricism does
not stop at insisting on the need for experiment in all disciplines
bearing on questions of fact (psychology, etc.); everyone is agreed
on this point. It adds a particular interpretation of experience,
whether that of the scientist or that of the human subject in general
(the object of the given psychological and sociological studies), by
reducing this experience to a mere record of observable facts instead
of finding there, as in other epistemologies, an active structuration of
objects, all of them related to the actions of the subject or to his attempts at interpretation. One result of this is that, in the field of the
psychology of learning and intelligence, investigators of the empirical philosophical school naturally tend to underestimate what has
been stressed by others under the name of the subject's actions; thus
it comes about that several theories of learning envisage the acquisition of knowledge as a kind of copy of reality and give the major
emphasis to external "reinforcements" that strengthen associations,
while nonempirical theories stress the factors of internal organization and reinforcement.

In the field of logic, which, as will be seen later (in Chapter 6),
cannot be entirely dissociated from psychosociological factors, logical empiricism has been led to present logico-mathematical structures
as the expression of mere language, as general syntax and semantics,
while authors not attached to this school see in natural logic the unfolding of operations that thrust their roots as far as the general coordination of actions at a level much deeper than that of language.

These conflicts between philosophical schools, due to ideological
influences, are yet sometimes fruitful, and more helpful than harm-
ful to the development of the sciences of man.[15] It is certain, for
example, that American theories of learning, inspired by empiricism,
played a positive role, first by pushing to its extreme limits a type of
interpretation that it was worthwhile to exploit thoroughly, and then
by encouraging a number of studies on neglected aspects of this
form of association. Similarly, logical empiricism, by dissociating
synthetic or experimental judgments too brutally from analytical or

[15] This does not exclude certain difficulties arising from the existence of "schools"
within the disciplines.

logico-mathematical judgments, provoked reactions from the logicians (like W. V. Quine) or psychologists, whose studies have enriched our knowledge even in terms of the problems raised by the empiricists themselves when they sought to place logico-mathematical constructivism in doubt.

In short, this first example sheds immediate light on the advantages and dangers of philosophical or ideological influences. The drawbacks would doubtless predominate if there were uniformity among the various trends or an absence of discussion and cooperation among the schools. As long, however, as we are dealing with problems formulated in terms of possible verification through experiment or formalization, knowledge can only benefit from contrasts that, as always in science, represent factors of progress.

II.

This leads us to the dialectical philosophies, which play a fundamental part in socialist ideologies, particularly in the fields of sociology and economics, and in a general way in all disciplines involving the dimension of historical development.

The case of dialectics, however, is rather different from that of empiricism insofar as, where the latter rightly stresses the importance of experience, it already gives it an interpretation unacceptable to nonempiricists; whereas when dialectics reveals the specific nature of historical developments, with their continual conflicts, oppositions, and excesses, it often limits itself to revealing mechanisms that anyone could accept; for the dialectical spirit is doubtless broader than attachment to any given school.

In contemporary dialectical movements, it is in fact possible to distinguish two currents, which we shall call immanent or methodological dialectics and more general or philosophical dialectics.

Spokesmen for the first of these currents see dialectics as an epistemological attempt to elucidate common characteristics (or, on the contrary, characteristics conflicting from one case to the other), all scientific efforts to assess developments taking place in time. Dialectics thus understood means therefore taking stock of methods of interpretation actually used in certain biological, psychogenetic, economic, and other studies. Being respectful of facts, dialectics may then often converge, even closely at times, with the concepts of authors who neither have nor wish to have any understanding of philosophical dialectics. For example, Pavlov, whose work was so significant in the arena of Soviet dialectics, often repeated that he knew nothing whatever of that philosophy—which was of no importance since his work involved a methodology of actions that others undertook to comment upon speculatively. In the psychology of psychogenetic development, studies on the launching of intellectual operations on the basis of preoperative and sensorimotor regulations, on the role of imbalance or contradictions and restoration of balance through new syntheses and extensions—in short, all the constructivism that characterizes the progressive constitution of cognitive structures—have often been related to dialectical interpretations without there having normally been a direct influence. Obviously such parallels may be used by followers of methodological dialectics that only attempt to clarify the trend of the sciences of development without interfering with the sciences themselves; and this work of comparison and epistemological reflection can only be helpful to them.

It has, however, also been possible since the time of Kant and Hegel to conceive a philosophical form of dialectics that, like many other philosophies, sometimes seeks to found or even to direct the sciences. In such a case, it ceases to be anything more than one system of interpretation among many. Nevertheless it has been of very great importance, for in the case in point, it can base itself on a tested methodology that coincides with the spontaneous methodology of many disciplines, as has just been recalled. The only problem of interest to us, then, is that of correspondence between ideas and facts.

The influence of philosophical dialectics has been translated into concrete form in the fields of sociology and economics, and it is undeniable that Marxist dialectics has exercised a very great influence in this respect. It is interesting to note here, because this study bears essentially on the trends of the sciences of man and is not designed to offer a doctrinal synthesis, that one can in the present state of things distinguish three types of attitude toward a movement of this kind. Some people see Marxist dialectics as an expression of the dominant truths at present accessible in the sociological field. Others believe the contrary and see in it just one of several interpretations with no presently demonstrable superiority. Yet others consider it a "metasociology" of obvious interest for guidance (clearly the best available) in research work, but offering no possibility of experimental verification, and lying in the field of mere interpretation.

III.

A third example is of quite a different kind: that of phenomenology; that is, a philosophy that does not claim to lead to scientific research or to elucidate the methods of already constituted sciences, but rather to parallel these sciences themselves by offering a truer understanding of the realities under consideration.

With reference to this group of tendencies (of which Bergsonism was an earlier example), one should observe at the start that conflicts between the sciences and some philosophies have existed only since the nineteenth century, at a time when some philosophers dreamed of a speculative power that would permit them to encompass Nature itself (cf. Hegel, in his *Naturphilosophie*), and when, conversely, certain thinkers maintained that they could derive scientific metaphysics from their positive knowledge (as in dogmatic materialism) and thus provoked reactions in the shape of systems designed to protect moral values from such encroachments, which they regarded as unwarranted. As a result, the critique of science (in the sense of epistemological reflection) frequently led various philosophies to set frontiers to scientific knowledge (as intended, incidentally, by the positivist doctrines) and to try to set up, beyond those frontiers, another type of knowledge tantamount to a duplication of science itself in this or that scientific sphere.

The point is of great importance because, in the final analysis, it raises the question whether science is "open-ended" or whether there are fixed and definitive frontiers that by their very nature separate scientific from philosophical problems. This second solution has thus been that chosen by positivism, which, in the time of Comte, made the establishment of laws a prerogative of science, but removed from its orbit the search for causes believed inaccessible, and which today claims to confine the sciences to a description of observable facts and to the use of logico-mathematical terminology, surrendering to metaphysics other questions regarded as "imponderable." Further, and under quite a different aspect, Husserl's phenomenology seeks to reserve for science the study of the "world" of time and space, while nevertheless admitting, beyond this fixed frontier, an "eidetic" type of cognition, one of forms and essences, deriving from metaphysical intuition.

As a result of successive revolutions in physics, which have modified some of our most basic intuitions to the advantage, not of skeptical relativism, but of a relational objectivity of increasing efficacy, the general tendency of the sciences is to regard themselves as "open-ended" in the sense of an ever-present possibility of revision of concepts or principles, or even of problems themselves. No basic scientific notion has remained unchanged throughout history and transformations have even led to successive reformulations of logic as such. It would obviously be somewhat pointless to attempt to draw up unchanging frontiers to designate one class of notions as the only scientific one while considering another as purely philosophical. If so, it may be equally presumptuous (at least one notices an increasing tendency to think so) to draw definitive frontiers, or merely stable ones, between scientific and philosophical problems. A problem remains a philosophical one as long as it is considered solely on a speculative basis, and as has been seen in Chapter 2, it becomes scientific as soon as it can be defined with sufficient precision for methods of proof—whether experimental, statistical, or algorithmic—to permit a certain convergence of mind as to its solutions, not merely as opinions or beliefs, but specifically as precise technical research.

This being the case, a parascientific philosophy such as phenomenology naturally incurs the risk of remaining dependent upon the given state of the sciences that it seeks to criticize. Husserl (following Bergson) attacked the empirical and associationist philosophy that was prevalent at the turn of the century and rightly revealed its inadequacies. But instead of working to correct and perfect it, he accepted it as such and merely sought to mark out its frontiers so as to erect beyond them another form of knowledge dependent only on "intentions," meanings, and intuitions. Between the two, however, psychology has evolved and has become greatly enriched, to the extent that today the problem appears in quite another light. In consequence, such problems as that of the liberation of the logical intelligence with respect to the "world" of time and space (phe-nomonological "reduction") are today examined in the field of the psychology of development by verifiable methods; while phenomen-logical intuition seems to logicians even more tainted with this "psy-chologism,"[16] which had to be opposed, than does the work of the psychologists themselves. In short, if philosophical psychology of a phenomenological type could momentarily influence some individual writers (as in the case of the founders of *Gestaltpsychologie,* which incidentally took a clearly naturalistic course), it in no way modified the major trends of contemporary scientific psychology, which has pursued its own course of development.

[16] By "psychologism" is meant the unwarranted deduction of a law from a fact.

6

The Sciences of Man, the Natural Sciences, and the System of Sciences

The relationship between the sciences of man and the natural sciences is one of the questions most affected by ideological and even national influences. In areas where metaphysical speculation is least indulged in, such as the Anglo-Saxon countries and the popular republics (with due regard to the differences that oppose empirical and dialectical trends), this problem, if raised at all, is very much less acute: it goes without saying that psychology, for example, is seen in these countries as belonging both to the natural sciences and to the social disciplines. But among peoples more responsive to the lure of metaphysics, such as the Germanic (apart from the Viennese, with their traditional positivism) or Latin peoples, many doctrines have stressed the difference between *Naturwissenschaften* and *Geisteswissenschaften,* and psychology has usually been linked with philosophy. It is interesting to note that during the social sickness that overtook Germany until the end of the Nazi period, the conflict in question was worked up to a climax, and that during the entire Fascist period the teaching of psychology and scientific sociology was suspended in German and Italian universities (in the latter case, in spite of the very closely related political views held by V. Pareto) and only resumed afterwards.

I.

Some support for making a distinction between the sciences of man and the natural sciences can, of course, be found in the epistemological and methodological difficulties stressed in Chapters 3 and 4.

But as we have already seen, not all of these difficulties are peculiar to the sciences of man, and the problem of experimental objectivity does not offer only two extreme solutions—depending on whether scientific research deals with physical objects at our level or with man in society—but opens up a whole range of successive approximations, according as the physical phenomena are studied at different levels, and in particular according as we move from physiochemistry to biophysics and biochemistry, from there to the true biological disciplines, thence to psychology, and finally, only in the last resort, to the sciences dealing with human societies as complete structures. On the other hand, and above all, the methods employed give rise to more and more frequent exchanges between the natural sciences and the sciences of man. We shall enlarge on this point shortly.

The main reason for opposition between these two groups of sciences lies in the role and attributes of the "subject," and this is why the degree of opposition depends upon the extent to which the cultural circles in which the sciences of man are studied are swayed by the attractions of metaphysics. For the unshakeable champions of *Geisteswissenschaften,* seen *sui generis,* the "subject" is not a part but an observer and sometimes even a creator of nature, whereas for supporters of continuity, the fact of man's subjectivity is a natural phenomenon among others and does not prevent the subject from dominating or from modifying nature, nor from carrying out all the activities that traditional philosophy assigns to "subjects." This is the full range of the problem.

However, since the times when it was sought to oppose the subject and nature, and to make of this conflict a field of study reserved to those sciences of the mind that were closer to metaphysics than to those known as "natural" sciences, many changes have taken place in the evolution of the sciences in general, so that current trends, while stressing the specificity of problems at all levels of reality, are far from favoring a mere dichotomy.

A first fact to be noted—and it is fundamental—is the evolution of biology, the present contributions of which are of great importance in the interpretation of the formation of the "subject." The neo-Darwinism of the beginning of the century saw in the evolution of the organized being the resultant of two fundamental factors to which the animal as a subject was wholly foreign: firstly, random variations or mutations (as opposed to recombinations of the common genetic pool of the population, on which increasing emphasis is being laid today), and secondly, a selection imposed by the environment but conceived as an elementary weeding-out process leading to the survival of the fittest and the elimination of the others. The behavior of the animal was thus seen only as a very secondary factor, which had some effect on survival but no essential causality. We are led to believe today, on the contrary, that selection is basically related to phenotypical variations, themselves interpreted as "responses" of the genome to environmental pressures (Dobzhansky, Waddington, etc.). Now the phenotype already includes behavior, since both are of an adaptive nature. In addition, selection is understood today to include feedbacks and reverse actions: the organism selects and modifies its environment as much as it is influenced by it. But among other things, the selection and modification of the environment depends on behavior, which is seen as a factor of increasing importance in the process of evolution. In addition, objective research has been carried out (J. Huxley, Rentsch, etc.) on the concept of "progress"—which was rejected by formal neo-Darwinism after the excessive optimism of the early days of the theory of evolution—and the criteria used naturally referred also to behavior. For all these reasons, animal psychology or ethology plays an increasingly vital part in zoological biology, while botanists insist more and more on reactive processes. Animal psychology already gives us a fairly impressive picture of the stages of learning and intelligence from the level of insects and cephalopods to the level of human life; in a very stimulating study, K. Lorenz has shown how modern theories on the instincts could be extended in an aprioristic interpretation (K. Lorenz is a Kantian!) of the principal categories of human thought. Without necessarily adopting this solution, it is in any case impossible today to consider the "subject" as detached from nature, since the most general trends in biology and ethology are to consider behavior and organic life as closely linked, and to study the animal as a subject.

II.

A second area in which the natural sciences and the sciences of man meet is through the exchange of methods. We stress the word "exchange," for it will be seen that the service is reciprocal.

In the first place, it goes without saying that the sciences of man are increasingly led to use statistical and probabilistic methods, as well as abstract models elaborated in the field of the natural sciences.[17] One single example of these logico-mathematical structures, owed to the natural sciences, which have been of service to the sciences of man, is the well-known convergence between the concepts of entropy in physics and in the theory of information. At a first glance there would seem to be nothing less likely to create a link between disciplines so far removed from one another as thermodynamics and linguistics. But in working out a mathematical theory of information and in comparing the structures of the expressions used to define an increase of information in relation to "rumors" and disorder, it was discovered that, from an essentially formal point of view and in relation to the symmetries involved, a certain isomorphism between these functions and those used in research on entropy did actually exist. In such a case, the techniques acquired in a natural science threw a clear light on those that had to be worked out to solve a difficult problem of central interest to the sciences of man.

Supporters of the specificity of the *Geisteswissenschaften* can naturally argue that such examples, however numerous they may be, prove nothing, but simply point to the "naturalistic" attitude to be found more and more frequently, and according to them mistakenly, in the sciences of man. But there is an answer to this, and a very good one, for it is the sort of argument likely to reassure those who fear that the concept of the originality of superior human behavior may be weakened by such parallels. It so happens, and increasingly, that the sciences of man, merely borrowing the broad general model that combines logico-mathematical deduction and experiment from the natural sciences, are led to build up certain new logico-mathematical techniques to meet their own ends; and that these techniques—intended for strictly "human" purposes—have in many cases been found to cast new light on the natural sciences and to throw up unexpected solutions to points that "natural" scientific techniques had so far been unable to elucidate. In other words, if there is a trend to "naturalize" the sciences of man, there is also a trend to "humanize" certain "natural" techniques.

[17] This point is developed in *Main Trends in Interdisciplinary Research*.

A first example of this may be found in the theory of information, which, after drawing its formal inspiration from thermodynamics, had a reverse effect on the interpretation of the discipline, to such an extent that L. de Broglie could consider the bringing together of the problems of entropy and information as one of the most fruitful and stimulating discoveries of the last decades. Moreover, one cannot open any contemporary work on biology without continually encountering problems of information, from the codification of genetic information in the spiral order of DNA (deoxyribonucleic acid, the constituent of the genome) to the problems of conserving acquired knowledge or "memory" (this term alone reveals the trend we have already mentioned towards humanizing elementary processes), which memory probably presupposes the indivisibility of RNA (ribonucleic acid, which has a fundamental part to play during the whole epigenetic process, including phenotypical adaptations).

Another very striking example is to be found in the "theory of games" or decision, which has been adapted to the needs of econometry by Von Neumann and Morgenstern. This technique, which has proved increasingly useful in the study of human behavior (from perception with Tanner to moral behavior with Braithwaite), has also had its effect on the natural sciences, as the following two examples will show. The first is to be found in the well-known problem of Maxwell's demon in thermodynamics, of which Szilard had already worked out a very promising reformulation about forty years ago and on which a rational theory based on the notion of its "information cost" can be put forward today. The second belongs to biology, in which problems of economics are in fact constantly arising: Ashby has shown recently that one of the simplest models for biological or nervous regulation can be based on "strategics" and on an implication chart based on the theory of games.

Cybernetics as a whole, dealing as it does with problems of communications, as already mentioned, and of guidance, today constitutes an essential link between physics and biology. It cannot perhaps be seen, from this point of view, as emanating directly from the sciences of man, since man is sometimes more interested in guiding his robots than himself. But he does sometimes give thought to directing his own conduct, and it cannot be denied that human guidance played its part in the construction of cybernetics. One has only to reflect in this context on the evolution of the idea of finality. It is well known that finalism in its rather crude Aristotelian form covers a system of notions inspired by deliberate human action and therefore qualified as anthropomorphic in accordance with Cartesian and classical reasoning. But if the idea of finality is still obscure, the problems of adaptation, of functional utility, of anticipation, and so on, raised by finalism remain entire; and in discovering the "mechanical equivalents of finality," in elaborating a "teleonomy" distinguished by its rationality from teleology in its usual meaning, cybernetics has made an essential contribution both to the sciences of man and, through reverse action, to the natural sciences (in this particular case, to biology as a whole).

III.

Cybernetics is a first example of a discipline that is difficult to place accurately between the natural sciences and the sciences of man. There are many other examples, and this is a third argument of growing importance in favor of continuity.

It should first of all be noted that the sciences usually contrasted with the sciences of man and grouped together in faculties of sciences are generally known as the "exact and natural sciences." What does the term "exact" mean? It is often applied to physics, for there is a branch of physics called mathematical physics, but it is evident that no experimental science, even theoretical physics, can be anything but approximative. The word "exact" is therefore mainly applicable to mathematics. But can these sciences then also be "natural"? If one simply wishes to convey that they are concerned with nature, one must then concede that they are also concerned with man—otherwise they would not be natural in the sense that they would simply be drawn from physical experience, whereas they go very much further and include an internal need that is quite foreign to that experience. To say that mathematics is exact means therefore that it is one with logic; but there would be no logic without man, even though logic itself is rooted in the requirements of the biological structure.

The problem becomes more acute in respect of logic itself. In its present form, logic is an axiomatic and algorithmic discipline closely connected with mathematics and often taught as mathematical logic in faculties of science. As such, it therefore belongs to the exact and natural sciences, and apart from its truly mathematical applications, it is frequently used in physics and even biology (Woodger). From this point of view, it is no more than a working technique comparable with the theory of groups or with algebra in general, and therefore constitutes a "subjectless logic" that seems to have no further bearing on the sciences of man. But already in the field of scientific logic or of scientific theory as such, logic cannot be entirely dissociated from the logical subject. First, the logic of language or general syntax calls for a metalanguage or system of meanings, and this necessarily concerns the human subject. In addition, the considerable research carried out on the limits of formalization, resulting from Goedel's theorems (1931), also raises the problem of the subject, for here it becomes necessary to explain the impossibility of reducing all phenomena at one stroke to a formal expression, and the need for constant efforts to improve upon original theories, moving from "weaker" to "stronger" theories, without once remaining content with mere points of departure.

But above all, beyond the logician's logic, we have to take into account the logic of the subject in general. For if logic is axiomatic, it stands to reason that it must be so in terms of a preexisting reality of a given nature that it is logic's task to render axiomatic. Now this given nature cannot be reduced to elements in the subject's consciousness but must also stem from the operational structures used by him, of which he is only partly conscious but which underly his own actions and reasoning. In the same way as certain "natural numbers" are present in prescientific enumeration and are later used as the arithmetical basis for a theory that goes far beyond them, there are also certain natural logical structures (classifications, seriations, accordances, and so on) which the subject draws and builds upon in his spontaneous activities and which the logician himself uses in his work of formalization.

Now the logico-mathematical structures of the subject are also studied in the psychology of development in cultural anthropology or in sociology itself, in that branch styled the sociology of knowledge. We cannot therefore dissociate logic from the sciences of man, since the logic of the logician constitutes a formalized and highly enriched extension of the logic behind the subject's activities. This human aspect of the structural and operational sources of logic is indeed so deep that it can now be traced back, beyond general and even sensorimotor coordination that provokes action, to nervous coordination. McCulloch and Pitts have pointed to the isomorphism that exists between operative structures intervening in various forms of neuronic connections and the operative factors of propositional logic (Boolean system), and this important discovery indicates that if logical complexes are the result of progressive structuring, reorganized and reinforced from one level to another up to the stage of formalization itself, these structures, although not predetermined but gradually developed, can be traced back to nervous and sensorimotor acts of coordination.

In short, logic belongs both to the exact and natural sciences and to the sciences of man, and provides links between them all that defy linear classification. But if this is accepted, it must be admitted that the same applies to the scientific forms of epistemology itself. Epistemology has classically been considered as a branch of philosophy, but two new kinds of facts today indicate trends toward autonomy similar to those that marked the gradual achievement of autonomy by psychology, sociology, and logic.

The first range of new facts is that the epistemology of each of the advanced sciences is the fruit of research carried out by its own specialists. The problems of the bases of mathematics, for instance, are increasingly dealt with by mathematicians themselves, taking account mainly of logical, but also frequently of historical and strictly psychological, considerations (Poincaré, Brouwer, Enriques, Gonseth). The epistemological theory of physical experience, particularly since the revolutionary onset of microphysics, is elaborated by practicing physicists. In biology, an attempt at epistemological formulation by L. von Bertalanffy resulted in a movement known as the "general theory of systems," which endeavors to single out the epistemic mechanisms common to the various disciplines involved, including psychology, and so on.

The second series of facts is that certain methods of approach in epistemological research are oriented toward the study of development. Theorists of knowledge have long since realized that the historical analysis of the formation of ideas and methods, known as the "historicocritical method," throws light on the mechanisms of scientific knowledge. Studies such as those of A. Koyré or T. S. Kuhn, for instance, are extremely instructive from the point of view of the epistemology of physics and chemistry, and a study of the history of mathematics led L. Brunschvicg and P. Boutroux to carry out searching epistemological analyses. But history does not give us all the answers, and beneath or beyond the historical plane, there is psychogenesis and sociogenesis. T. S. Kuhn himself, for instance, refers explicitly to my research on the child as if it were what Brunschvicg had already done, thus showing that when the historian acts as an epistemologist, or vice versa, he could benefit from a knowledge of psychology.

Generally speaking, all scientific epistemology, whether connected with perception, language (as related to thought), or operational structures, refers implicitly or explicitly to psychological interpretations. But in the place of psychology, of a summary and sometimes speculative type, one might conceive of a corpus of research aimed at the experimental control of the various psychological hypotheses involved in the many epistemologies of number, space, time, and so on. This task, known as "genetic epistemology," is in fact being carried out systematically by an interdisciplinary team of research workers who call upon the assistance of development psychologists, logicians, and specialists of the disciplines involved in respect of each epistemological question. It cannot then be denied that this movement partakes in the sciences of man, although the research may be undertaken on the epistological aspects of the exact and natural sciences. Here again, epistemology emerges as a link between the two groups of disciplines.

If, finally, we try to place the sciences of man within the scientific system as a whole, the preceding comments show that it is impossible to confine ourselves to a mere linear classification.

A model for these linear classifications was provided by A. Comte, who arranged the sciences in the order of their increasing complexity and decreasing generality. Such a series, applied to our present problem, would work out roughly as follows: mathematics, physical sciences, biological sciences, psychology, and lastly, the social sciences in their interdependence. But here the problem of situating logic becomes immediately evident. Comte himself did not attempt to solve this problem, no doubt because modern symbolic logic had not taken shape in his day; but he often speaks of "natural logic" either to dwell on its role in the constitution of mathematics, or more implicitly, by regarding it as a product of collective life, which amounts in effect to placing it in the field of social realities (and the later "logical positivism" links it explicitly with linguistics in its more general aspects). Now, if logic has some connection with the human subject, and we have seen above that there are sound reasons for accepting this ideal today, it will therefore belong to the fields lying at the end of the series, while still playing a fundamental part in mathematics that is at the head of the list—which leads one to the conclusion that the linear order is an illusion and that we are in fact moving in a circle.

In reality, none of the sciences can be displayed on a single plane, for each involves hierarchical levels: (a) its object or the material content of study; (b) its conceptual interpretation or theoretical technique; (c) its epistemology or analysis of its bases; and (d) its derivative epistemology or analysis of relations between the subject and the object in relation to the other sciences.

If we deal only with level (b), and possibly (c), that is, with theoretical techniques of sciences and their internal epistemology, the linear order in question is wholly acceptable and logic must be placed at the head of the list, for logicians do not consult psychologists or even linguists to assist in working out their axiomatization; mathematicians must submit to the demands of logic, but not to those of physics or biology, and so on.

On the other hand, as soon as we come to consider the object of disciplines, namely, (a), and their derived epistemology (d), it becomes clear that the object of logic cannot be entirely separated from the subject insofar as logic formalizes operational structures built up by the latter; and the order of the sciences must become circular once again.

This circularity is indeed extremely interesting when we study the epistemology of the sciences of man, for it reflects the fundamental circle that characterizes the interaction of the subject and the object: the subject is aware of the object only through its own activities, but can learn to know itself only through its action upon the object. Physics is thus a science of the object, but it reaches the object only through the intermediary of logico-mathematical structures resulting from the activities of the subject. Biology is another science of the object, but the living being it studies, using instruments borrowed in part from physicochemistry, is at the same time the starting point of the behavior pattern of a subject that leads to the human subject. In studying the latter, psychology and the sciences of man use some of the techniques of the earlier sciences, but the human subject also builds up logico-mathematical structures that provide a starting point for the formalizations of logic and mathematics. In sum, the scientific system as a whole is caught up in an endless spiral, the circular motion of which has no negative effects in itself but simply gives expression to the dialectic between subject and object in its most general form.

One thus sees that the sciences of man, while remaining the most difficult and complex, occupy a privileged position in the scientific circle: as sciences of the subject that itself builds up the other sciences, they cannot be separated from these others without being artificially simplified and distorted; but if the human subject is put back in his proper place, which is at the same time that of a culmination in the perspective of the physical and biological object, and of a creative starting point in the perspective of action and reflection, the sciences of man alone render the closing, or rather the internal coherence, of this circle of sciences intelligible.

7

Major Theoretical Trends:
Forecast and Explanation

I.

Insofar as the sciences of man cannot be isolated but are part of the whole complex of sciences, and insofar as this complex assumes a generally circular or spiral form, the problem that dominates the main theoretical trends is assuredly that of the specificity, or on the contrary, the reducible character, of the phenomena studied in the different branches of science; for if the concepts of interaction and interdependence are gradually taking the place of linear series or simple genealogical structures, the question naturally arises whether the trend is toward general assimilation or toward relational or dialectical modes of interpretation in which both oppositions and analogies are taken into account.

This is no mere academic question, but a very real problem. In psychology, there is a tendency to reduce observable facts to physiology on the one hand and to sociology on the other, while overlooking the specificity of the mental factor. In sociology, there is a tendency to reduce behavior to a scale close to that of social psychology or to economics, linguistics, and so on, without paying attention to the specific objects proper to sociology—the overall forms of society. Broadly speaking, wherever we find differences of scale—for in the sciences of man as well as in the natural sciences, it is the scale that creates the phenomenon, as Ch. E. Guye so penetratingly observed—the problem is to determine whether mechanisms on a higher scale can be reduced to serve on the lower ones, or whether the former simply cannot be reduced, or again whether there is any intelligible relation between the two.

This problem is commonly met with in the natural sciences. Laplacian determinism was a dream of integral reducibility such that the whole universe, in its innumerable manifestations, could be reduced to a basic equation from which all others would be derived. A. Comte, however, despite the linear form of his classification of the sciences, considered each stage to be marked by some irreducible concept; for instance, he opposed the reduction of chemical affinity to the laws of physics. In fact, however—except where there has been simple reduction (that is, the discovery of identity beneath apparent dissimilarity)—the problem of reduction in the physicochemical sciences usually leads to circular causality through reciprocal assimilation. Einstein, for instance, was able to do without the Newtonian force of attraction at a distance by reducing the movements of the heavenly bodies to inert movements along the curves of Riemannian space. This geometrical concept of gravitation was accompanied by a physical concept of space in that the curves were regarded as being determined by masses. Similarly, after a period of attempts at reduction, the relations between mechanics and electromagnetism led to interdependence and progressions out of which came wave mechanics.

Obviously, in the sciences of man, while problems of this nature are constantly arising, although in quite different terms, the range of possible solutions is in general smaller, due to the lack of such highly developed logico-mathematical or even experimental techniques. Yet again we find the same triad—reduction, the specificity of phenomena at the higher level, and causality with retrogressive action.

An everyday example of this can be seen in the relations between language, which is a group mechanism and in that respect superior, and intelligence or thinking, which is restricted to the individual and in that respect lies at a lower level.[18] We need only point out here that, while the reduction of grammar to "reason" seemed obvious in the seventeenth and eighteenth centuries, the view that thought is subordinate to language prevailed subsequently and has continued to be held until very recently. Chomsky, however, to some extent returns to the classical position, but his discovery of transformational grammars makes it possible to analyze psycholinguistic

[18] This question is dealt with more fully in *Main Trends in Interdisciplinary Research*, section 16.

interactions much more thoroughly than heretofore, in conjunction with the psychogenetic study of the cognitive functions; in the present state of knowledge, therefore, it appears that intelligence comes before and conditions the mastery of language, although there are reactions within the process in which both innate and acquired knowledge is overtaken by a more general mechanism of progressive equilibration. We are therefore induced to move beyond the initial antithetic theses, and this presupposes a continual refining of the forms of causality employed.

II.

This brings us to the central problem of the laws and causes, or of forecasting and explanation. As we know, positivism has constantly insisted that science should be compelled to confine its attention to the discovery of laws or to forecasting based on laws, and to refrain from seeking for causes or "modes of production" of phenomena. It is strange that this restriction should have been made by Comte, who, rightly or wrongly, was convinced of the utilitarian nature of science—the more so since, although forecasting is useful to human activity, the latter is concerned primarily with producing rather than with reproducing, while for both these purposes the "mode of production" is far more important than is forecasting.

Specialists in the different branches of the natural sciences frequently call themselves positivists and make some statement to that effect in their prefaces, as if science were merely a matter of establishing and generalizing about laws and deducing from them certain predictions that can be verified by experimentation. But as E. Meyerson has ceaselessly pointed out, when we move on from the preface to the body of the work, we find a very different state of affairs, for no scientific thinker worthy of the name discusses laws and functions without seeking the reason for them, without trying to isolate "factors," and without introducing explanatory hypotheses as constituting basic ideas in research work. One of the best-known examples of the futility of prohibitions is to be found in atomic research, the hypotheses underlying which was severely censured by certain positivists while it was no more than an explanatory postulate; but we all know what atomic science has since achieved. It is true that if the atomic phenomenon is a causal model for phenomena at a higher level than itself, we find only laws, and not immediate causes, when we study the atom. But the laws in turn require an explanation, and so on.

The refusal to search for causes or for the mode of production of phenomena has undoubtedly had fewer repercussions in the human sciences, firstly because they are newer and more modest disciplines (and because the trends claiming to be "positivist" differ from each other still more than in other branches), but also—indeed primarily —because the prime function of man is to act and to produce, and not merely to contemplate and to forecast; so that while the need to understand and to explain is no more marked in the psychological and social sciences than in others (actually it is constant in all sciences), it is possibly more explicit and more conscious. It is true that, following upon Dilthey's reflections and Jaspers's psychopathology, some schools of thought are inclined to distinguish between "explanation," which they say is material and causal in nature, and "understanding," which in their view is concerned with conscious meanings and intentions. This, however, merely complicates the problem (see below, Section III). No one is thinking of questioning the need for explanation, and the very concept of "causality" is coming back into fashion in sociology as a result of the studies of "multivariate analysis."

But in what does explanation consist? In the sciences of man as in the natural sciences, the search for causality has three stages, only the last two of which throw light on explanation:

1. First comes the establishment of facts and laws, although these are not two separate problems, for a fact is only a relation that can be repeated. The establishment of a law is therefore nothing more than the recognition of the generality of the fact and of itself does not constitute an explanation. It is true that people often refer—though incorrectly—to "causal laws" in the sense of regular successions in time; but this so-called causal law is nothing but a law that, like any other, provides a basis for the search for causality; in itself it provides no explanation. Moreover, any law makes forecasting possible simply because it expresses statistical or completely determined regularity; but the

forecasting is merely an anticipation of a new fact in accordance with the general applicability of the law in question, and it too provides no explanation; it merely tells us that the fact is generally true. On the other hand, while the criterion of causality is the presence of necessary and sufficient conditions, there is an intermediate stage within the sphere of laws that leads to these relationships of necessity—the stage of functional dependence $y = f(x)$, or the determination of the variants of y in terms of the variants of x. In the case of multiple variants, therefore, we may legitimately acknowledge that there is a certain degree of causality in the role ascribed to the determining factors.

2. The second stage begins with this establishment of relationships —that is, with the deduction of laws. The difference between the necessity proper to explanation and the generality that is characteristic of laws as such is that the generality relates only to facts (no matter how complex are the inductive methods or, in other words, the probabilist or statistical methods that enable it to be established), whereas necessity is characteristic of logical or mathematical links; therefore, if we try to deduce laws instead of merely recognizing them, we are introducing an element of necessity that brings us nearer to explanation.

There are, however, two kinds of deduction. One is merely inclusive or syllogistic and is based solely on the relationship of "all" and "some"; from this sort of standpoint, a law A (for example, the law of perceptive or opticogeometric illusion as in Müller-Lyer's figure) may be deduced from a law B (the law of all opticogeometric illusions belonging to the category of "field effects," or what we have called relative centrations), simply because this law B is more general. In this case we are not going beyond the field of laws, and the deduction is nothing but a generalization, which brings us nearer to the explanation but also moves the problem further away. The other form of deduction, the only one that is explanatory, may be called constructive. It consists in introducing laws into a mathematical structure that has its own norms of composition, not by a simple interlocking process, as in a syllogism, but as a result of more or less complex transformations—for instance, a "network" structure, a "group" structure, or a loop system (regulations or feedbacks), and so on. In this case, the necessity for transformations joins the generality of laws and moves toward explanation.

3. Even a constructive logico-mathematical deduction, however, is only logical or mathematical, and does not deal with facts except by means of a third process, which is essential to the explanation. This is the construction of a "model" adapted to fit the facts themselves—a model so constructed that deductive transformations can be made to correspond to real transformations, so that the model is the projection of the logico-mathematical pattern into reality, and thus consists of a concrete representation based upon the real modes of composition or of transformation that can be expressed in terms of the pattern. A cybernetic circuit, for example, is not merely a matter of equations—it amounts to the identification of the details of the supposed feedbacks in the facts. Of course, in that case, facts will lead only to the recognition of laws, but laws on different scales; and the model consists in putting them together to form a coherent system that corresponds, term for term, with deduced or deducible mathematical transformations. In a word, the model is explanatory insofar as it enables us to give the objective processes themselves a "structure" that is itself isomorphous.

We are thus led back to the classical rationalist interpretations of causality, not simply as mere regular successions as in Hume's empiricism, but as the reason for things (*causa seu ratio,* as Descartes said) or as an analogy between deduction from experience (Kant) and dialectical construction. Such questions as whether this causality relates to strict determinism or to probabilist models, and whether it reaches linear successions or always in fact moves towards loop systems or circular interactions, are unimportant details, for in all cases the characteristic property of causality—that it is a deductive construction that is part and parcel of the real—remains, thanks to the inexhaustible wealth of experience and the limitless fecundity of logico-mathematical structures.

III.

At this point, however, a problem peculiar to the human sciences inevitably arises—the problem of the interpretation of the facts of consciousness as opposed to material facts—and this brings us to the general question of understanding (*Verstehen*) as opposed to explanation (*Erklären*).

Psychologists are familiar with the problem, which is that of the relation between consciousness and the body. Two classical solutions to this problem have been put forward—that of interaction and that of parallelism or isomorphism. The first regards consciousness as being or possessing a kind of power that can act on the body, just as the body can act on consciousness. The difficulty here is that properties peculiar to matter (work, strength, energy, and so on) are attributed to consciousness and such attribution, theoretically speaking, makes it difficult to uphold the principle of the conservation of energy[19] in cases where this intervention of consciousness occurs in physiological mechanisms; such attribution cannot be verified experimentally because what we observe is the action of the physiological concomitants and not the action of consciousness as such. It should be noted that the numerous positive data collected by so-called psychosomatic or (according to the ideology adopted) corticovisceral medicine prove nothing about this, for they merely show the effect of mental life (including both consciousness and higher nervous activity) on organs regulated by hormones and nerves; they do nothing to show how consciousness as such acts independently of its nervous concomitants.

The second solution is that of psychophysiological parallelism or isomorphism. According to this view, consciousness and its organic concomitants are the two aspects—inner and outer—of a single reality, but there is no possible causal interaction between these aspects, which are the two possible expressions of a single reality. We may express them in terms of idealism, materialism, or duality of nature,

---

[19] Or the second principle of thermodynamics, since consciousness would in that case lead to the choice of the least probable of the possible material developments (but it is precisely this antientropic action that some defenders of interaction try to bestow upon it).

as we wish. This solution is logical, but the objection to it is that we can no longer perceive the function of consciousness, which merely accompanies certain material processes and produces nothing itself.

We have therefore suggested a third solution. It is only an epistemological generalization of the second, but it endows consciousness with a cognitive activity *sui generis*. If we analyze the relations between states of consciousness, we perceive the essential fact that they are invariably due not to causality proper, in the sense given above, but to another kind of relation, which might be called implication in the broad sense of the term. Essentially, a state of consciousness expresses a meaning, and one meaning is not the cause of another meaning, but implies it (more or less logically). The concepts "two" and "four," for instance, are not the cause of the proposition $2 + 2 = 4$, but they imply it of necessity, which is not the same thing; and although we can obtain 4 from 2 and 2 on a calculating machine, this causal product is not a state of consciousness unless the user attributes meanings to it and expresses it in the form of conscious implications. To put it briefly, consciousness, in our view, is a system of implications (between concepts, affective values, and so on), and the nervous system is a causal system, while psychophysiological parallelism is a special case of isomorphism between the implicatory and causal systems. This view restores a specific function to consciousness.[20]

The duality between the facts of consciousness and those of material causality is constantly evident in the social sciences proper, and while some sociological systems, such as Weber's, stress the phenomenological aspect of the former, others, such as Marxism, do not accept explanations unless they also cover material facts.

We have therefore reached a point, especially with Jaspers's psychopathological studies, at which we have two quite different broad types of interpretation—those based on the "understanding" of conscious intentions and meanings, and those based on "explanation" by material causality. But although this distinction is valuable and even

---

[20] It should be noted that this solution adds nothing to the "parallelist" models as regards particular psychophysiological facts. But from an epistemological standpoint it has the advantage, as we shall presently see, of placing the question within the much wider problem of the concordance between implication (logico-mathematical) systems and physical (as well as physiological) realities.

highly relevant, there is no fundamental opposition between the two types; we have already seen why, when discussing the artificial conflicts that some authors have tried to create between the *Geisteswissenschaften* and the natural sciences. In fact, if we are prepared to adopt the hypothesis that there is a parallelism between implication and causality, in the general sense just mentioned, we have here a case of complementarity rather than a fundamental opposition, and this complementarity, in different but comparable forms, recurs even in the natural sciences: whereas mathematics deals rather with implications, which must simply be "understood," without looking for any causal explanation, physics has to do with material facts, which must be "explained," and the parallelism between conceptual implication and material causality is therefore so close that causal or explanatory models establish an increasingly close relationship between implicative and material sequences. Very broadly speaking, the sciences of man are moving in a similar direction; in other words, they are all trying to understand *and* to explain, but not to understand without explaining or to explain without understanding.

There are many other questions on the main trends in the theory of the sciences of man that could well be dealt with in this chapter, but they will be dealt with elsewhere.[21]

---

[21] In *Main Trends in Interdisciplinary Research*.

8

Specialization and Integration;
Basic Research and Applications

Progress in any field of study is obviously a matter of differentiating between problems and theories and of establishing integrating relationships within the field of study or between it and other closely related disciplines. But this spontaneous development, which seems almost biological and is the direct result of the laws of structuration applicable to intelligence in its intra- and inter-individual operations, becomes complicated owing to numerous sociological and sometimes even ideological factors, not to speak of epistemological considerations, that are usually bound up with the spontaneous trends of evolving science but that may act as special factors, either accelerating or hindering progress.

I.

The general sociological factor that complicates the natural specialization process in the sciences of man and often produces marked hindrances instead of advantages is the creation of "schools" in the true meaning of the term, within the disciplines themselves, with the inevitable isolation and danger of dogmatism.

This phenomenon is probably peculiar to the sciences of man, for what we have also referred to as "schools" in the natural sciences are rather trends of thought connected with positions that are opposed so long as experimentation or deduction has not ended the debate. For example, the conflict between energeticists and atomists in physics at the end of the nineteenth century was an epistemological dispute rather than a war of schools, and the new facts discovered since then have united every shade of opinion. It is true that we speak of the Copenhagen school and the Paris school in contemporary microphysics, because of the great names of Niels Bohr and L. de Broglie, but the discussion whether the accidental is primary or derivative in nature, and whether an underlying determinism is impossible or in fact exists, is one of those discussions that are the result of a variety of legitimate interpretations awaiting ultimate agreement.

In the case of the sciences of man, the ideologies themselves imply the existence of opposing schools, which is perfectly natural, and often leads to fruitful discussion. We need not go back over this, but it should be noted that the phenomenon is sometimes much more widespread, and that specialization by schools still occurs at a much lower level than that of the great ideological conflicts. It may be useful, therefore, to give one or two examples, which we shall select in the realm of psychology as the most experimental of our branches of study.

A typical example is that of the various schools of psychoanalysis. Freud discovered a number of new facts and interpretations, but they were not immediately accepted because of their startling nature and of the new modes of thought implicit in Freudianism as distinct from current mechanistic schools of thought. But instead of trying to convince the psychologists and psychiatrists by moving into their usual field of discussion, which would have been possible if he had accepted the support of a number of like-minded thinkers such as E. Bleuler, Th. Flournoy, and others, Freud chose to work at the head of a team of ready-found disciples and to pursue his own path without making any systematic attempt to come to an understanding with others. Because of this scientific attitude, and also because they wished to protect their newly emerging techniques professionally, the Freudians founded an international psychoanalytic society whose members were all trained by itself. The advantage of creating an *espirit d'école* of this kind is of course that it enables specialists holding the same principles to progress without constantly going back to initial problems. But this has two disadvantages. First, if agreement is reached too rapidly, verification is neglected, and this is the aspect of psychoanalysis that mainly held back experimental psychologists who in other ways were interested in Freudian functionalism. Second, differences of opinion lead to the rise of new schools, and this is what happened with Jung and Adler. At present, the situation is evolving, and for two reasons. The first is that some psychoanalysts have become aware of the need for an experimental basis and for the linking of their theories with psychological theories in general; an example of this is the movement born of the work of D. Rapaport at Stockbridge. The second reason is that there is an increasing tendency among experimental psychologists to take over the main ideas underlying psychoanalysis rather than the details of Freudianism. The psychoanalytical "schools" persist nonetheless, but with a marked and significant tendency to separate into individual "clans."

Another example of a different kind is found in the tendency noticeable for some time in American behaviorism to belittle research work that is under suspicion of "mentalism" or that refers more or less directly to the consciousness of the subject. Behaviorism was brought to light by Watson, but is parallelled in similar trends in many other parts of the world besides the United States (cf. Soviet psychology with Pavlov, or French psychology with Piéron). The basic method advocated by behaviorists in studying a subject is to start from the subject's behavior as a whole and not simply from his introspection. Seen from this standpoint, the internal mechanisms of thought appear to be essentially the product of the interiorization of actions themselves—of speech, once it is interiorized, or of sensorimotor actions, and so on. But the characteristic feature of the behaviorist school in its early days was to deny the very existence of thought, except as a complex of verbal meanings, and to proscribe any reference to consciousness. Thus theoretical extrapolations from a methodology valid in itself became the characteristics of the development of this type of school, and it is easy to understand that it may have been very advantageous to emphasize the differences rather than the similarities between research workers in order to get the most out of a new methodology. Since then, however, positions have become more flexible, and the very fact that the "behavior theory," as it is called today, has the allegiance of the vast majority of research workers shows that it covers a wide range of possible shades of opinion, so that it is no longer correct to speak of it as a "school" in the proper sense of the term. As we have seen above, when Tolman, for instance, says that "expectation" is one of the basic factors of the learning process, it is difficult to see how this notion differs from mentalist concepts. On the other hand, when Skinner declines to have recourse to intermediate variables and regards the human organism as an "empty box" of which nothing is known except its inputs and outputs, he is applying the behaviorist rules strictly, but he is doing so from methodological prudence and not necessarily any longer from an *esprit d'école;* for he well knows that the research work of the future will move in the direction of filling this "box" with both physiological and psychological elements.

An even simpler way in which a "school" may be formed is by isolation (which is sociologically comparable to the biological factor that produces new species on islands lying at a distance from any continent). A mechanism of this kind can be seen at work in contemporary research in social psychology. This branch of psychology arose from the discovery of new and entirely legitimate problems— the problem of the possible effect of group interaction on mental functions that at first glance appear to be independent of it (perception, and so on), or the problem of the dynamics of interactions in small social groups, for instance. But while the best writers on social psychology are closely in touch with research work in experimental psychology in general, and so produce some very valuable syntheses (cf. a recent work by R. Brown entitled *Social Psychology*), many "social psychologists" immure themselves totally within their own chosen ground. In such cases, scientific specialization is likely to be accompanied by the formation of a "school," which is the product of an ordinary psychosociological artifact.

II.

Whereas the emergence of schools in this way usually has the effect of increasing specialization, although as a result of the impact of more or less extrascientific factors, the opposite may also happen— some schools may aspire to greater integration than that achieved by spontaneous intra- or inter-disciplinary coordination. They may succeed to some extent, but once again, out of pure *esprit d'école,* they oppose other possible integrations, which might have been more natural in some cases and more comprehensive in every case.

Once more we may take as an example the logical positivism that issued from the "Vienna circle" (in which the psychosociological factor is fairly clear, for the Viennese have always had a special talent for organizing this sort of intellectual society). In this case, the goal of the school is explicitly "the unity of science," an ideal that recurs in the title of the *Encyclopaedia for Unified Science* and in that of the Institute that Ph. Frank established at Harvard; and this unity is sought by reducing scientific data either to observable facts ascertained perceptively, or to the formulation of an accurate vocabulary, that of logic and mathematics. But what the opponents of logical positivism have against it is that, on the contrary, it lacks this unity, for two reasons. The first is the profound rift it creates between the facts of experience and the logico-mathematical vocabulary, whereas in linking logico-mathematical structures with the actions and operations of a subject, we achieve greater unity in the relationship between subject and object. The second reason is that in reestablishing the activities of the subject, we attain a more constructive conception of the sciences, which renders them more "open" instead of enclosing them within the classical barriers prevalent in all forms of positivism. Hence logical positivism, which is a source of integration for some, appears to others as bound up with a "school" inhibiting the desired integration.

Other movements that are not so obviously a school also strive to promote the integration of scientific research. We have already referred to the interesting movement begun by L. von Bertalanffy called the "general theory of systems," which covers both the human and the natural sciences. Its object is to try to discern the theoretical structures that are common to all attempts at synthesis, whether in biological organicism or in the interpretations of overall data in sociology and psychology. A movement of this kind is in fact allied to all the trends toward the mathematization and especially the cybernetization of the sciences that are concerned with mental or social organic life.

III.

The twofold trend toward specialization and integration, which is the result of movements of ideas and problems, but which, as we have seen, is accompanied by various sociological stimuli, interferes in some ways with the spontaneous division of work into basic research and tentative application. This is a question of the greatest importance in relation to the present study, for the reason why UNESCO undertook its survey of the main trends in the sciences of man[22] is obviously that they are useful to society and will be increasingly useful in the future.

We thought it desirable, however, to deal with this problem in conjunction with that of specialization and "schools," not only because the dominant element in the latter is often the desire to apply a theory, but also because the frequent isolation of practical workers from theoretical research may have the same disadvantages as those manifest in separation into schools—disadvantages that are then all the more serious because they reduce the efficiency of practical work.

The relations between basic research and the many attempts at application are profoundly different in those branches of study in which experimentation in the strict sense is possible, and in those that deal with scales of phenomena in which the statistical and probabilist analysis of observable factors rules out experimentation. In the latter case, application plays an important part because it really acts as a substitute for experimentation. The classic example of this second type is economics: when an economist is asked to organize a particular test, the specialist makes a number of forecasts based on theory, and the ensuing events confirm or disprove them in the same way as experimentation would, except that it is not always possible to isolate all the factors. Accordingly, this kind of application is bound up with basic research, and one could list a number of outstanding writers, who, like Keynes, were both theoreticians of the first rank and the instigators of numerous practical experiments. In such cases, it is obvious that application draws the *maximum* advantage from the progress of basic research, since it stimulates the latter.

Branches of study such as psychology, in which basic research work can be pursued using experimental methods without necessarily having recourse to application, are quite different. Nevertheless, experimental psychology has given rise to a large number of

22 *Main Trends of Research in the Social and Human Sciences,* 2 vols. (Paris and The Hague: Mouton/Unesco, 1970), in which this essay originally appeared as the Introduction.

applications almost since its beginnings, and great writers such as Binet have initiated both important basic research (on intelligence, for instance) and widely used practical processes (such as his intelligence tests). Obviously, the main reasons for this are that any psychological theory concerns human life and that circumstances are such that psychologists are constantly being called upon to solve some practical problem or other. But another reason may be found in the example of medicine, with which psychology has always been closely related, and which owes a good deal of its information to the study of applications, although its bases lie in general physiology and biology.

We must therefore draw a distinction between two problems regarding the relations between basic research and application in psychology: the problem of the contribution made by the latter to the former, and that of the contribution made in the opposite direction. These two problems, however, are relatively linked, and in the last resort are such as to cast doubt upon the very idea of "applied psychology" from the standpoint of both its theoretical interpretation and the advantages of application for its own sake.

On the whole, these applications of psychology have contributed little to psychological knowledge itself, except in the sphere of pathological psychology, in which disease is a kind of natural experimentation (for instance, the dissociation of the speech factor in aphasia, and so on), and applied research assumes a heuristic value, similar to what we saw in the case of economics. But in the other spheres it would be impossible to cite a discovery that was due to application; Binet, for instance, deduced nothing from his tests related to the interpretation of intelligence. Yet, as we have seen, "applied psychology" is almost as old as psychology, and could have contributed to the development of the latter. But for this very reason, it did not always succeed in taking advantage of the basic research work that would have been useful to it, because it evolved too early and because it constantly sought to apply the knowledge gained in a particular sector before the subject had been thoroughly investigated. Consequently, attempts were made to evaluate achievements and results before the formative mechanisms were known, and the result was often mutual impoverishment.

In addition, there have been the effects of the formation of "schools." Applied psychology organizes its own congresses and has a tendency to become a kind of state within a state, with all the disadvantages of relative isolation in science. To take the sphere of application alone, this means necessarily limiting the scope of problems, and those that would ultimately be the most interesting to resolve, for the sake of application itself, are sometimes neglected because, in their initial form, they appear to relate only to basic research or theory.

We stress this example because it is most instructive, especially in comparison with the way in which applications are made in the natural sciences. As we know, the applications in physics, chemistry, and biology, which are altogether more valid, have often occurred in the most unexpected way as a result of basic research, and sometimes even of purely theoretical research totally unrelated to practical application. An example that has often been quoted is the role of Maxwell's equations in present-day applications of electromagnetics. But if we confine ourselves solely to application and try, for instance, to measure a subject's intelligence before we understand what intelligence is in general and how it evolves, the applications we make will be much more limited than those that we could expect to make once we had understood the formative mechanisms.

In short, there is no such thing as "applied psychology" as an independent branch of study, although any sound psychological study will lead to valid applications. Broadly speaking, the function of the sciences of man is to provide increasingly valuable applications, in all spheres of knowledge, but on condition that basic research is developed without prior limitation imposed for the sake of utilitarian criteria; for what seems to be the least valuable at the beginning may have the most unexpected consequences, whereas initial delimitation with a view to practice makes it impossible to see all the questions at issue, and may result in neglecting what is in fact the most important and fruitful line of investigation.

74 75 76 77 78 79 80   12 11 10 9 8 7 6 5 4 3 2 1